Stripping & Finishing FURNITURE

RICHARD RUTHERFORD

MINI • WORKBOOK • SERIES

MEREHURST

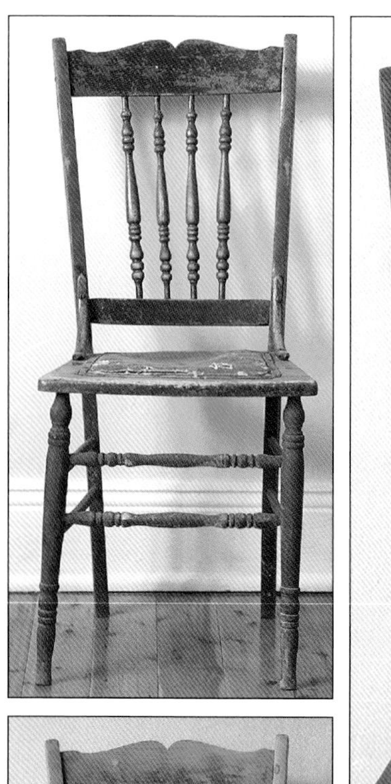

CONTENTS

An old kitchen chair (far left, top) was stripped and repaired (bottom), and then finished with acrylic paint (left).

BEFORE. The paint on this old school desk was chipped and scratched.

Stripping paint using paint stripper

One or more layers of paint can be stripped from furniture most efficiently by using a chemical paint stripper. This heavily painted desk was an ideal candidate for its use.

EQUIPMENT

- Paint stripper and old paint brush
- Gloves; safety goggles; face mask
- Paint scraper
- Skarsten scraper
- Abrasive paper: nine sheets of medium and three of fine grade
- Orbital sander
- Cork sanding block
- Tack cloth or clean rag

METHOD

1 Using an old paint brush, apply paint stripper to the piece, a section at a time. Different brands of stripper have different requirements, so check the instructions and follow the safety instructions carefully. Wear gloves and safety goggles, and make sure the area is well ventilated.

2 Using the paint scraper, remove all loose and soft paint from the surface.

AFTER. Any finish applied to the desk now will adhere strongly.

Use the Skarsten scraper for grooves and tight areas. Remove excess stripper with water or white spirit as instructed; allow to dry.

3 Sand all over the piece, using the orbital sander for any large flat areas and the cork sanding block for tighter ones. Start working with the medium abrasive paper and work up through the grades to the finest until all areas are sanded clean and smooth.

4 Wipe the piece with the tack cloth to remove any residue. For the refinished desk, see pages 34–5.

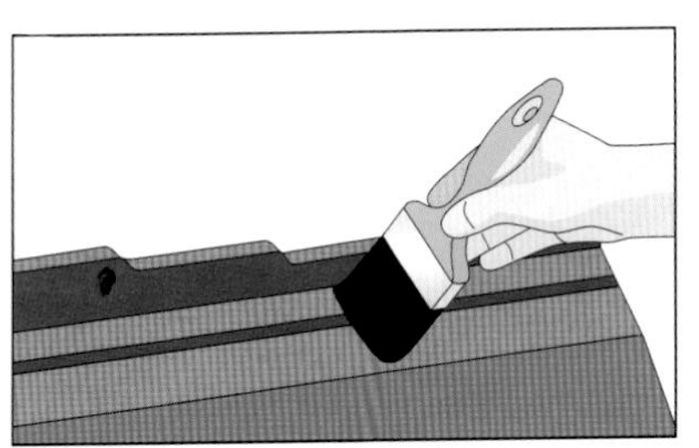

1 Use an old paint brush to apply stripper. Follow any safety instructions on the container carefully.

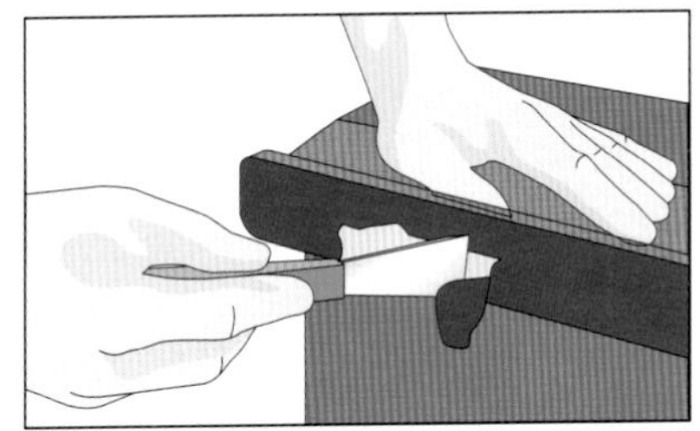

2 Use the paint scraper to remove all the loose and softened paint from the surface, including corners and edges.

***BEFORE.** This dresser with stained glass panels is a beautiful piece of furniture but it bore evidence of its long life in the paint that partly covered the original varnish.*

Stripping paint using a hot-air gun

If you decide not to use chemical strippers, there are a number of mechanical ways to remove old paint and varnish from furniture. Scrapers and steel wool can be used but you need to be careful not to gouge the surface of the wood. On this dresser we used a hot-air gun to soften the paint before scraping.

METHOD

1 Hold the nozzle of the hot-air gun 5–10 cm (2–4 in) from the painted surface. The distance will depend on the thickness and type of paint: the paint should bubble and blister without burning. As the paint bubbles, lift it away with the paint scraper. Continue until the majority of the paint is removed.

HINT

Before beginning work, remove any doors, drawers, latches and hinges. This may not always be possible (except for the drawers), but it will make the job a lot easier and the finished item will look more professional.

EQUIPMENT

- Hot-air gun
- Paint scraper
- Abrasive paper: eight sheets each of medium and fine grade
- Orbital sander
- Gloves; safety goggles; face mask
- Cork sanding block
- Skarsten scraper
- Triangular shavehook
- Tack cloth or clean rag

2 Starting with the medium abrasive paper, sand the whole piece. You will save time and effort if you use an orbital sander for large, flat areas but you can use abrasive paper wrapped around the cork sanding block.

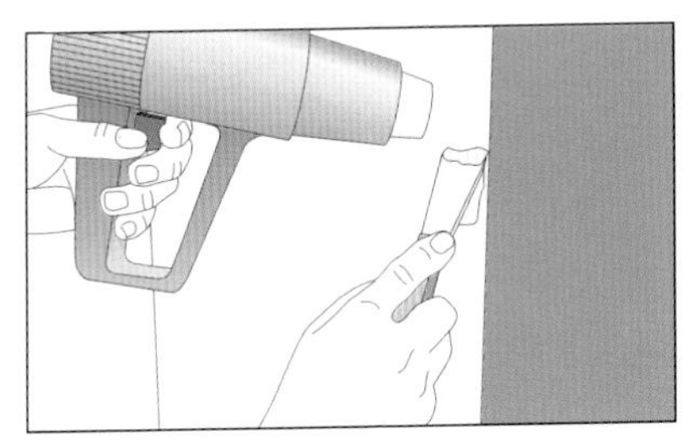

1 Hold the nozzle of the hot-air gun 5–10 cm (2–4 in) from the surface and scrape the paint away as it bubbles.

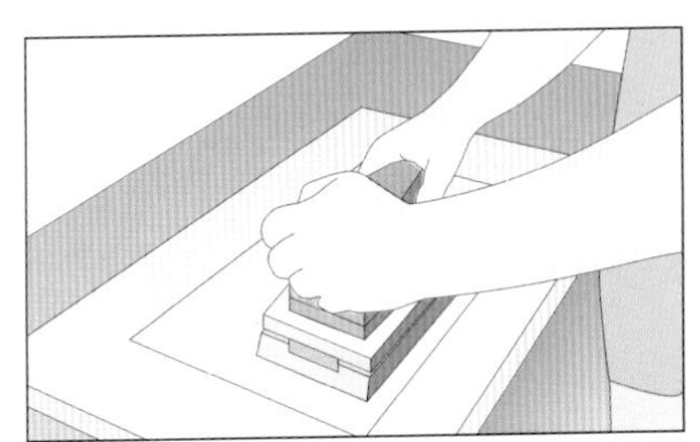

2 Sand smooth the item. Using an orbital sander on large flat areas will save you a lot of time.

USING SKARSTEN SCRAPERS

To use a Skarsten scraper, hold it firmly and pull towards you. Push the scraper away from you only in exceptional cases, such as when you are cleaning out grooves, as this can gouge the wood.

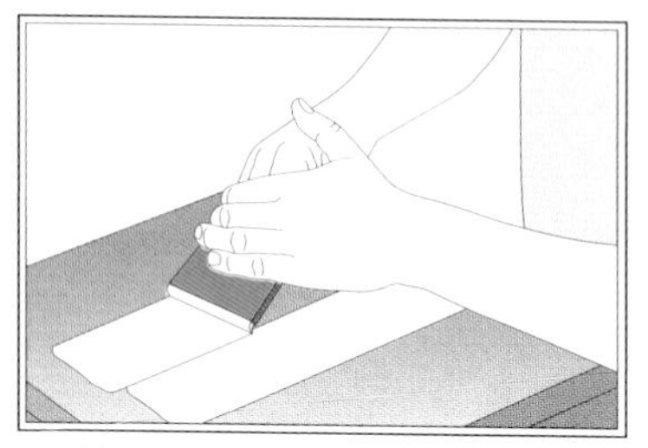

Hold the scraper firmly with both hands and pull it towards you.

3 Use the Skarsten scraper, the triangular shavehook and the cork sanding block to clean all corners and tight areas as you go. Work through both grades of abrasive paper until all the areas are clean and smooth.

4 Wipe over with a tack cloth or clean rag to remove any residue. For the refinished dresser, see pages 40–1.

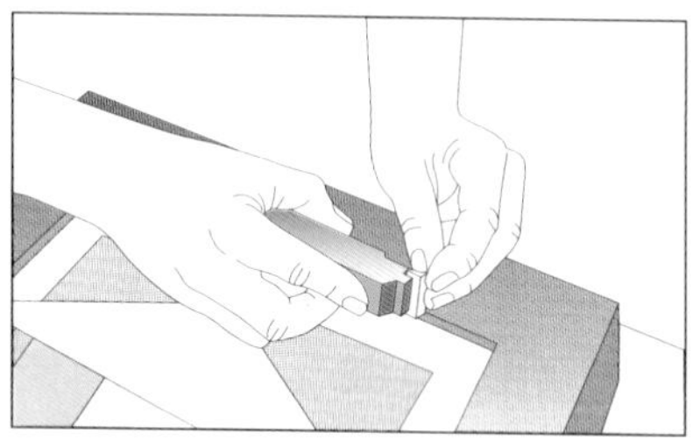

3 Use a scraper or abrasive paper to clean up corners and tight areas where paint remains.

LEAD PAINT

Paints used in houses and on furniture, especially primers and undercoats, contained very high levels of lead until about 1950, and some lead may be found in paints used after that. Stripping old paint can, therefore, result in considerable exposure to lead, which is particularly harmful to children and pregnant women. Pets can also be affected. If you are concerned, you can obtain kits to test whether lead is present from some paint suppliers.

The most dangerous methods of paint removal are abrasive methods as they produce tiny particles that can be inhaled. Blasting, burning, scraping and sanding should be avoided where paint could contain lead.

The best way to remove lead paints is with a chemical stripper, scraping the removed paint straight into a container for disposal. A heat gun can be used to soften very thick paint on flat surfaces provided the paint is not allowed to burn. Rinse the surface well with water to remove any residual dust.

Always wear protective clothing, including a face mask. Make sure children, pregnant women and pets are out of the house and avoid working on windy days when particles will be blown about.

***AFTER.** Stripped clean of the layers of paint and varnish, the dresser is ready to receive a new finish.*

BEFORE. *Thick, chipped paint covered this cast iron bedhead, hiding the details.*

Stripping paint from cast iron

Paint is removed from cast iron using mechanical methods: scrapers, wire brushes and abrasive paper. These methods will also remove any surface rust.

METHOD

1 Using the paint scraper, scrape off all the loose, flaky paint on the surface of the piece. Check for rust and scrape it off at the same time.

EQUIPMENT

- Paint scraper
- Gloves; safety goggles; face mask
- Wire brush or electric drill with wire brush fitting
- Abrasive paper (wet and dry): four sheets of medium grade
- Garden hose

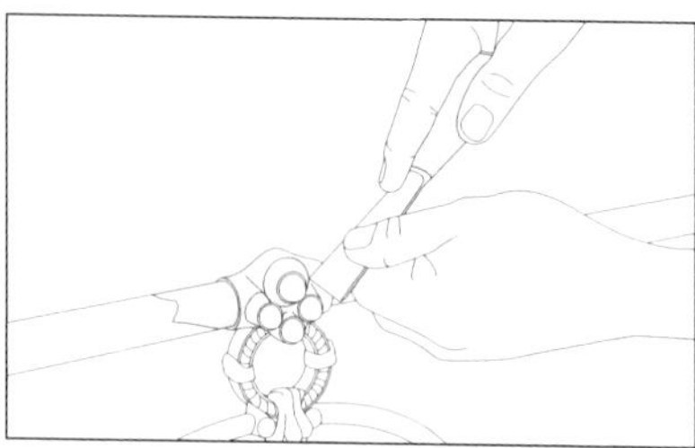

1 Use a paint scraper to scrape off all the loose paint and any rust that may have developed on the iron.

AFTER. Cleaned back to the iron, the bedhead is ready for finishing.

2 Using a wire brush, clean the paint from ornate, cast areas. If you have one, you may prefer to use an electric drill with wire brush fitting, or a combination of both.

3 Run a garden hose to the work area so that there is a continuous trickle of water running over the part of the piece being worked on, and rub the smooth, open surfaces with a sheet of abrasive paper, using several sheets of the paper.

4 Thoroughly wash the whole piece, and then leave it to dry completely before applying a new finish (see pages 42–3).

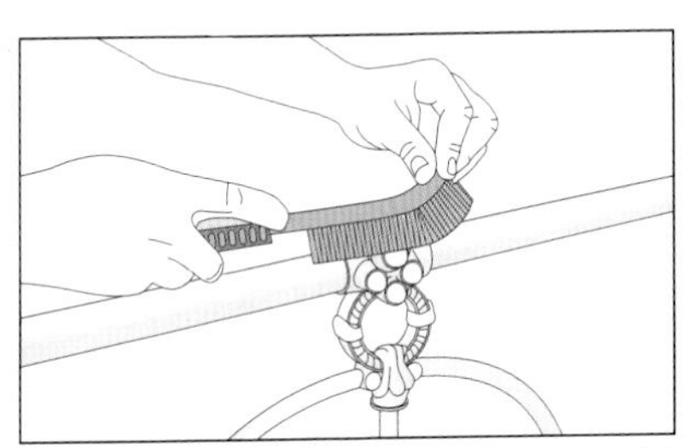

2 Clean paint from ornate areas with a wire brush, or an electric drill with wire brush attachment may be used.

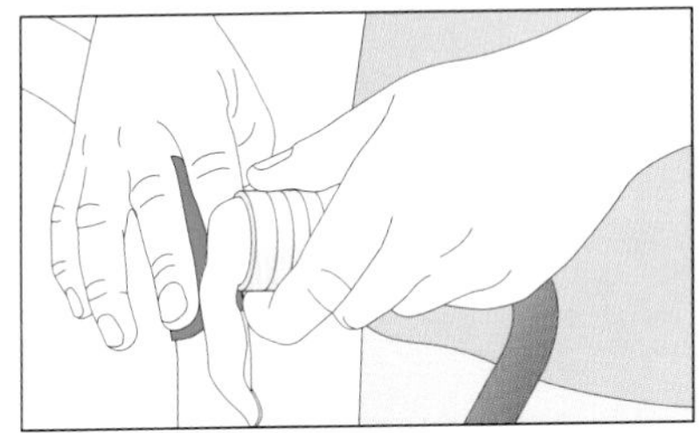

3 While dribbling water over the surface of the iron, rub the open areas smooth with abrasive paper.

Stripping paint from cane

Paint can be most easily stripped from cane or wicker using paint stripper, which can get into the tightest crevices.

EQUIPMENT

- Paint stripper and old paint brush
- Gloves; safety goggles; face mask
- Triangular shavehook
- Skarsten scraper
- Paint scraper
- Mild household detergent
- Wire brush
- Electric drill and flap wheel, medium (optional)
- Abrasive paper: four sheets of medium grade
- Soft brush or cloth

METHOD

1 Use an old paint brush to apply paint stripper until you see the paint reacting with the stripper. Make sure all crevices and corners are covered.

2 Scrape off the old paint. The triangular shavehook, Skarsten and

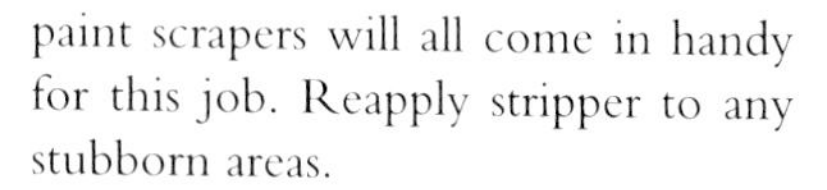

paint scrapers will all come in handy for this job. Reapply stripper to any stubborn areas.

3 Wash off the stripper with mild detergent and water, or white spirit (check instructions on can). If any remains, new paint will be affected.

4 Use a wire brush to remove paint from tight areas.

CLEANING RAW CANE

Unpainted cane furniture can be cleaned by washing with a soft rag and soapy, warm water. Leave it in the sun for several hours to dry thoroughly. The sunlight will also bleach the cane.

This furniture will be further bleached if it is washed with cold salt water or very diluted bleach and left in the sun.

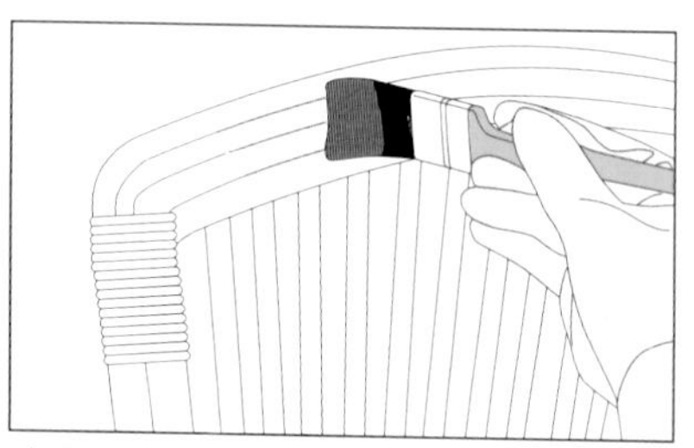

1 Use an old paint brush to apply paint stripper to all parts of the cane furniture. Pay attention to crevices.

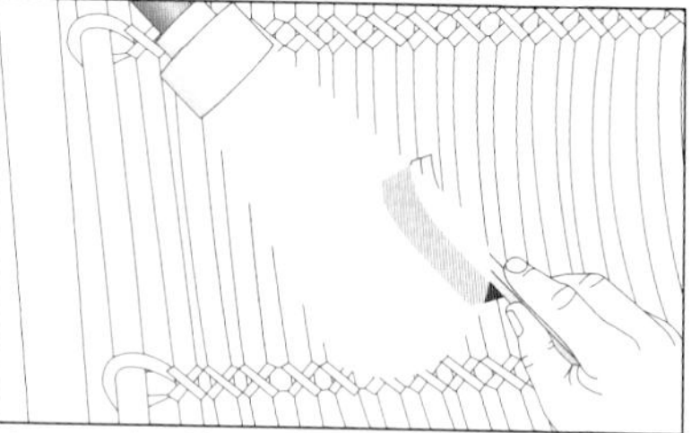

3 Wash off any residue of the stripper very carefully, or it may affect any new paint you apply.

***BEFORE.** Peeling paint, unravelling binding and a liberal covering of dirt made this cane chair an unattractive proposition.*

AFTER. Cleaned, repaired and stripped of its old paint, the chair is ready for its new finish.

REPAIRING CANE BINDING

Cane furniture is held together with cane binding and one of the repairs most often needed on this type of furniture is the replacement of unravelling binding.

1 Soak the new cane in water for about an hour to make it pliable.

2 Fix one end of the binding in place with a small nail, or a staple and PVA adhesive. Wrap it around as tightly as possible, using a spring clamp to hold it firm as you go. Finish the binding with a nail, or a staple and PVA adhesive.

Unravelling binding is a common problem on cane furniture.

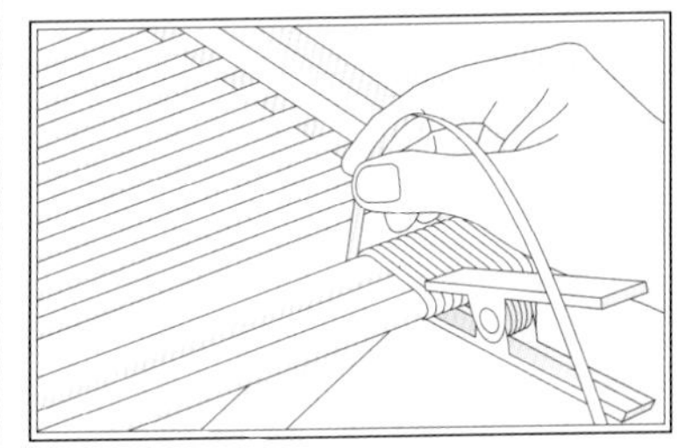

2 Bind the cane as tightly as possible, using a spring clamp to hold it as you go.

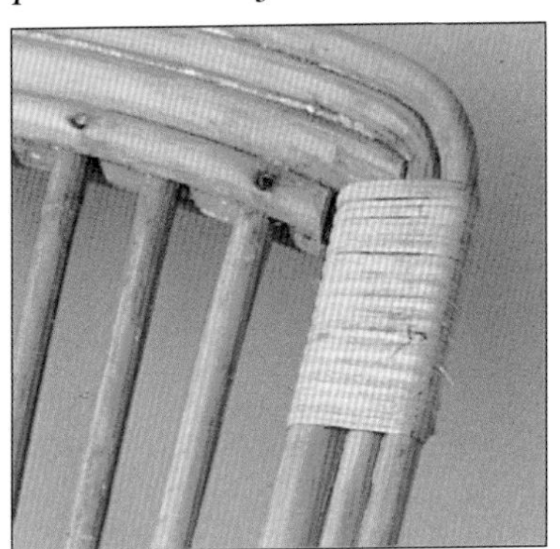

With new binding, the chair is now as good as new.

5 Using an electric drill and flap wheel with medium grade paper, sand as much of the piece as possible. Any areas that you can't get to will have to be sanded by hand with medium grade abrasive paper.

6 Dust off with a soft brush or cloth. Refinish as desired (see pages 44–5 for the repainted chair).

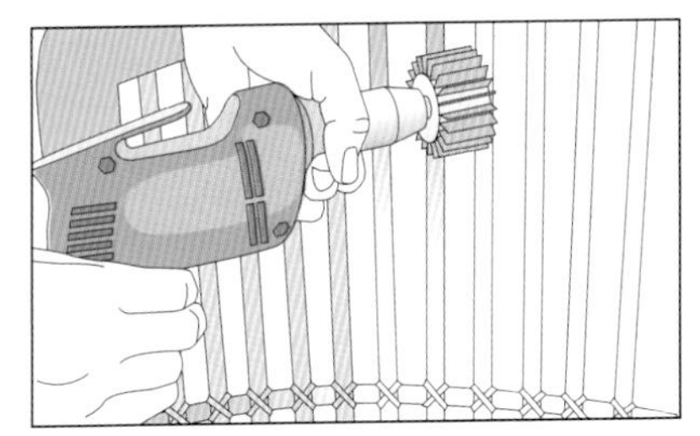

5 Sand the surface smooth, using an electric drill with a flap wheel if you have one or sheets of abrasive paper.

Stripping varnish with a scraper

Old varnish can be quite brittle, and when this is the case you can remove it easily by scraping alone. If the varnish adheres strongly to the piece, you will need to remove it by using a chemical paint stripper.

EQUIPMENT

- Skarsten scraper
- Abrasive paper: two sheets of medium, five of fine, one of very fine grade
- Cork sanding block
- Orbital sander
- Safety glasses and face mask
- Smooth file
- Wire brush
- Tack cloth

METHOD

1 Remove any handles or hinges.

2 Scrape off the varnish using a Skarsten scraper. Starting with the flat areas, scrape in the direction of the grain, usually with the blade at a right angle to the grain. If it's a little bumpy, turn the scraper 45 degrees and continue scraping with the grain.

3 Sand all the scraped areas with medium grade abrasive paper. This can be done using abrasive paper around a cork block or with an orbital sander.

4 Work on any decorative grooves or beads. Using the Skarsten scraper, with your fingers very close to the blade for support and control, scrape varnish out of the grooves. The scraper is normally pulled towards you but in grooves and tight spots can also be pushed away from you for effective cleaning.

5 Use a file with a good square edge to straighten the grooves and make them a bit deeper. Clean the file with a wire brush as you go along.

6 Sand large areas with the orbital sander, smaller areas with the cork block and abrasive paper, and grooves with folded fine abrasive paper. Dust off and wipe with the tack cloth. See pages 58–9 for the refinished chest.

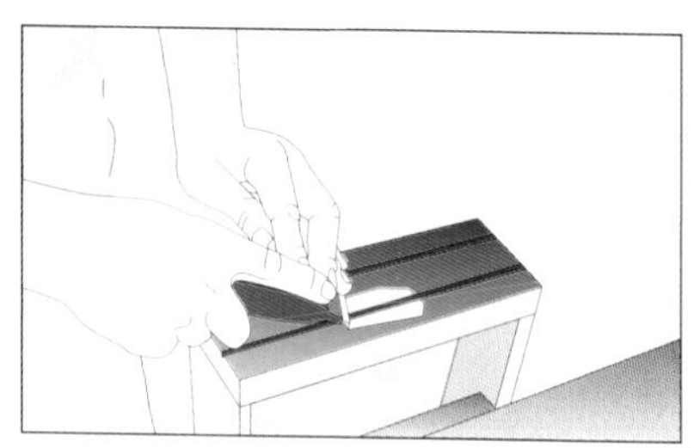

2 Scrape off the varnish using the Skarsten scraper, being careful to work in the direction of the grain.

BEFORE. Scratched and battered, the varnish on this miniature chest of drawers was brittle enough to be scraped off.

AFTER. The beautiful wood is revealed. A new piece of timber was shaped and glued to the broken corner (see page 31).

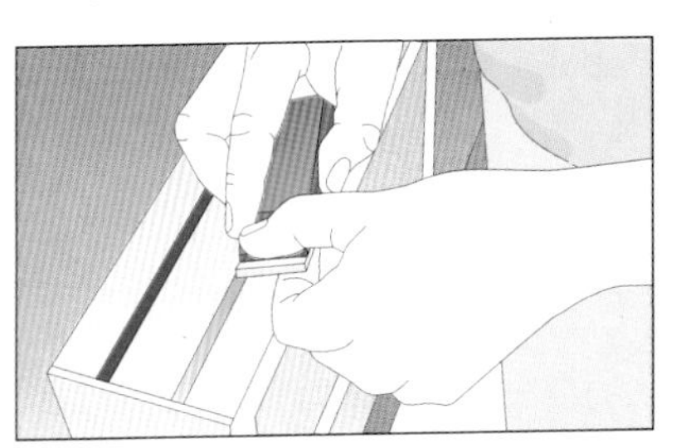

4 Use the Skarsten scraper to scrape out grooves. Hold it firmly close to the blade to control the pressure.

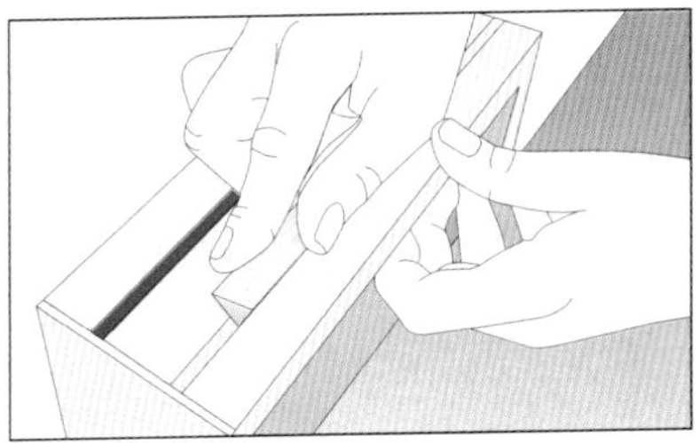

5 Use a file to straighten up any grooves, making them deeper and more regular.

BEFORE. *This classic chest of drawers had seen better days and required a new finish to spruce it up.*

Stripping varnish with paint stripper

Paint stripper can be used to remove old varnish as well as paint. It is the easiest method to use when the old varnish adheres well to the item.

METHOD

1 Using medium grade abrasive paper, sand the chest roughly to break up the existing varnish. This helps the paint stripper to penetrate.

2 Working in a well-ventilated area, lay down newspaper or plastic sheet where the stripped paint will fall. Wearing gloves and using the paint brush, apply the paint stripper liberally to all surfaces that need to be stripped. Leave until the varnish reacts with the paint stripper, by bubbling or lifting. This process can take anywhere from 1 to 4 hours.

3 Scrape off the softened varnish with a paint scraper. Any areas where the varnish doesn't scrape off the first time will need a second application of stripper.

EQUIPMENT

- Abrasive paper: six sheets of medium, eight of fine and four of very fine grade
- Newspaper or plastic sheet
- Gloves; safety goggles; face mask
- Old paint brush
- Paint stripper
- Paint scraper
- Mild household detergent
- Triangular shavehook
- Cork sanding block
- Orbital sander
- Soft brush or cloth
- Tack cloth

4 Remove any residue of the stripper. This can be done by washing the chest down with water

2 Brush on the stripper, giving all surfaces a liberal coating. Remember to work in a well-ventilated area.

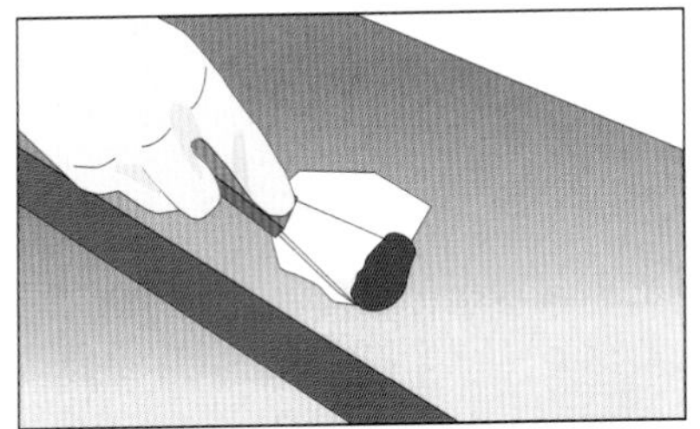

3 When the varnish bubbles or lifts, scrape it off. The stripper may take up to 4 hours to work.

Paint stripper was ideal for cleaning out these fine grooves.

and mild detergent, or white spirit as appropriate (check instructions). There is always a slight risk of damage when using water on timber, so on fine or valuable pieces you may use white spirit instead. Never put a wet timber item in the sun to dry.

5 Use the shavehook to remove any varnish in grooves or tight corners.

6 Sand the piece using the cork block and abrasive paper, working through the grades from medium to very fine. You may use an orbital sander for larger areas. Grooves can be sanded with folded abrasive paper. Dust off and wipe with the tack cloth. See pages 46–7 for the refinished chest.

SAFETY FIRST

SANDING

- Wear a face mask and safety goggles when carrying out any sanding procedure, and if a hazardous material (such as lead paint) is involved wear a special mask suited to the purpose.
- Wear ear muffs or ear plugs if using an electric sander or other electrical tools.

STRIPPING

- Chemical strippers can burn if they touch the skin. Wear goggles to protect your eyes, especially when scraping the paint off, and always wear gloves, long sleeves and trousers.
- Strippers can give off noxious fumes and should only be used in areas with plenty of ventilation.

STAINING OR PAINTING

- Always work in a very well-ventilated area.
- Wear protective, rubber gloves to prevent hands being stained.

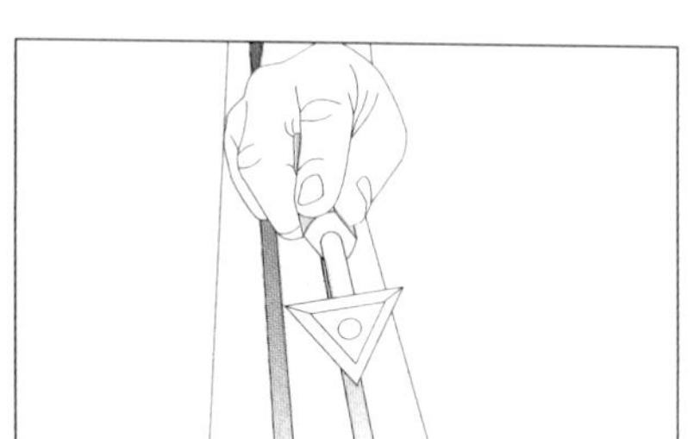

5 Use a triangular shavehook to remove varnish left in tight areas such as grooves or corners.

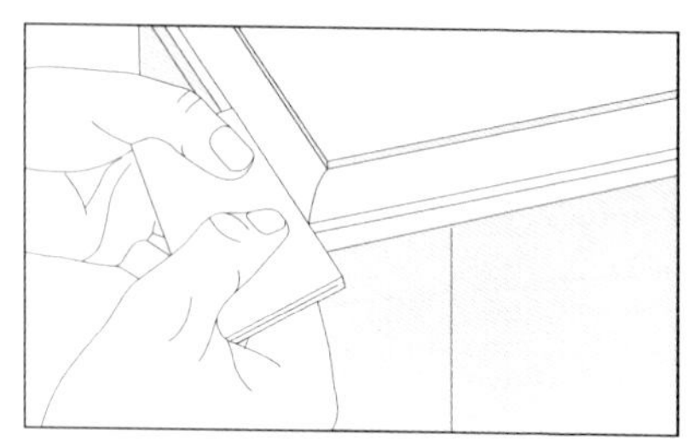

6 Sand the item, working through the grades of abrasive paper. Fold it in thirds to attack corners and grooves.

AFTER. Paint stripper easily removed the old varnish from this chest of drawers to reveal the beautiful timber.

Stripping a shellac finish

Shellac finishes, including French polish, are made by dissolving shellac in spirit. They are removed using methylated spirits, a process that is not difficult although it does require patience and a lot of rubbing.

METHOD

1 Apply methylated spirits to the surface of the item with the steel wool or nylon scourer (a nylon scourer may be easier to use as it won't clog up as fast). Be sure to wear rubber gloves. Rub backwards and forwards over a small section, rubbing with the grain as much as possible. Use a rag soaked with methylated spirits to rub off all excess shellac as you finish each section.

2 Using the Skarsten scraper, clean shellac from the grooves and corners. Use the file to tidy up any square, tight corners.

3 Starting with the medium grade abrasive paper, either wrapped around the cork block or folded to be easily manageable, sand all the grooves and corners on the piece. Work through the grades of abrasive paper except the finest, until the areas are sanded

EQUIPMENT

- Methylated spirits (about 1 litre for a small item)
- Fine steel wool or nylon scourer
- Rubber gloves; face mask
- Rag
- Skarsten scraper
- Smooth file
- Abrasive paper: six sheets each of medium, fine and very fine grade
- Cork sanding block
- Orbital sander
- Soft brush or tack cloth

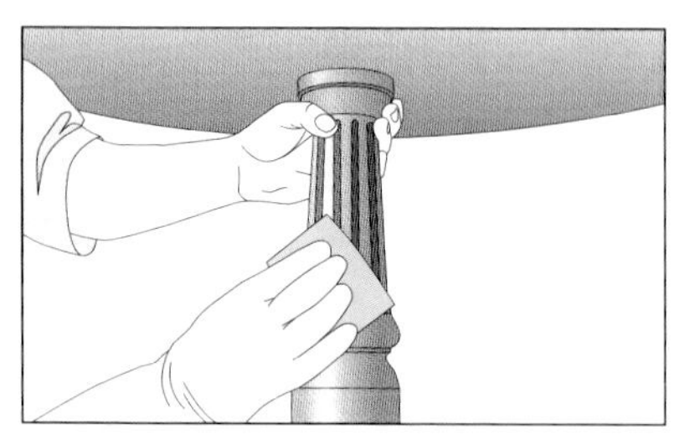

1 Use the steel wool or nylon scourer to apply methylated spirits. Wear rubber gloves to protect your skin.

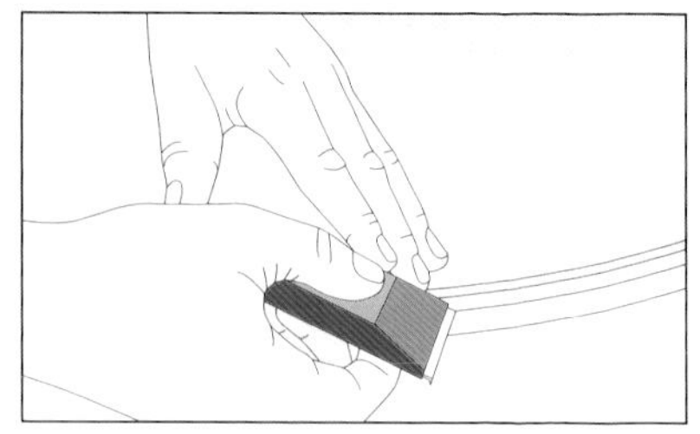

2 Remove shellac from grooves and corners with the Skarsten scraper. Work carefully to avoid gouging the wood.

***BEFORE.** The shellac finish on this table was scratched and very worn, especially on the top and around the edge of the base.*

***AFTER.** The shellac finish has been completely removed, showing how the table had been made from two different timbers.*

clean and smooth. You can achieve a reasonable finish using only three grades of paper (medium, fine and very fine) but using more grades gives a very fine finish, which is desirable if you plan to give the furniture a waxed, varnished or oiled finish.

4 Using either abrasive paper wrapped around the cork block or an orbital sander, sand the flat areas, again working through the grades of abrasive paper except the finest.

5 If you will be using a solvent-based finish, put the item aside for a while so that the moisture in the air can raise the grain. If you intend to use a water-based finish, the same effect can be achieved by wiping the item over with a dampened cloth.

6 When the piece is dry, give it a final sanding with the very fine abrasive paper.

7 Wipe the whole table with a tack cloth or soft brush to remove dust. The table was then given an oiled finish (see pages 60–2).

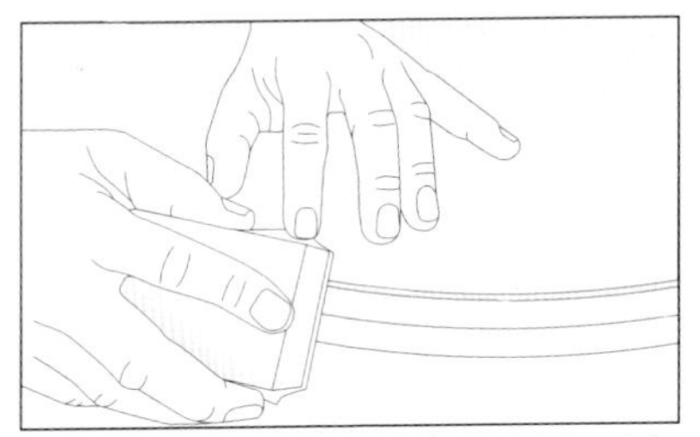

3 Sand the grooves and corners with abrasive paper wrapped around a block or folded so it is easy to hold.

SHARPENING SCRAPERS

A Skarsten scraper has disposable blades, but if you want to sharpen an old blade, hold the scraper in a vice at a 45 degree angle. Place a sharp file on the blade, positioning it to match the existing angle. Push the file over and across the blade so one stroke covers the whole blade.

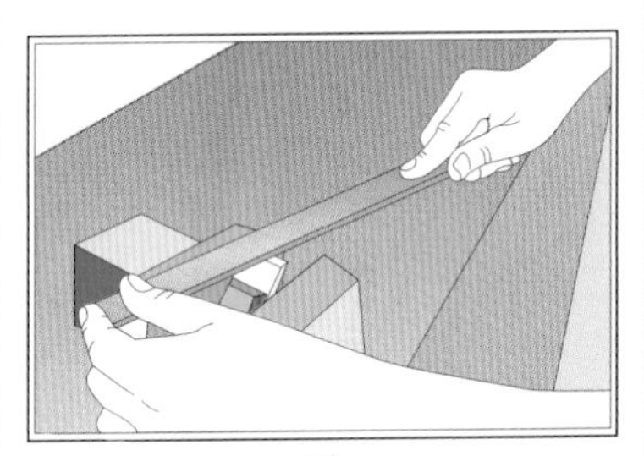

To sharpen a Skarsten scraper place it in a vice at 45 degrees.

To sharpen a triangular shavehook, place the metal shaft in a vice. Use the manufactured angle as a guide and push a file over and across the edge of the scraper. If the scraper is old and blunt you may need to regrind the edge on a bench grinder.

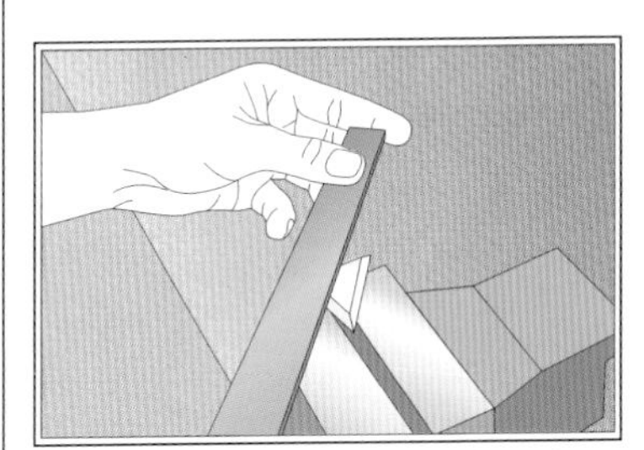

To sharpen a shavehook, place the metal shaft in a vice.

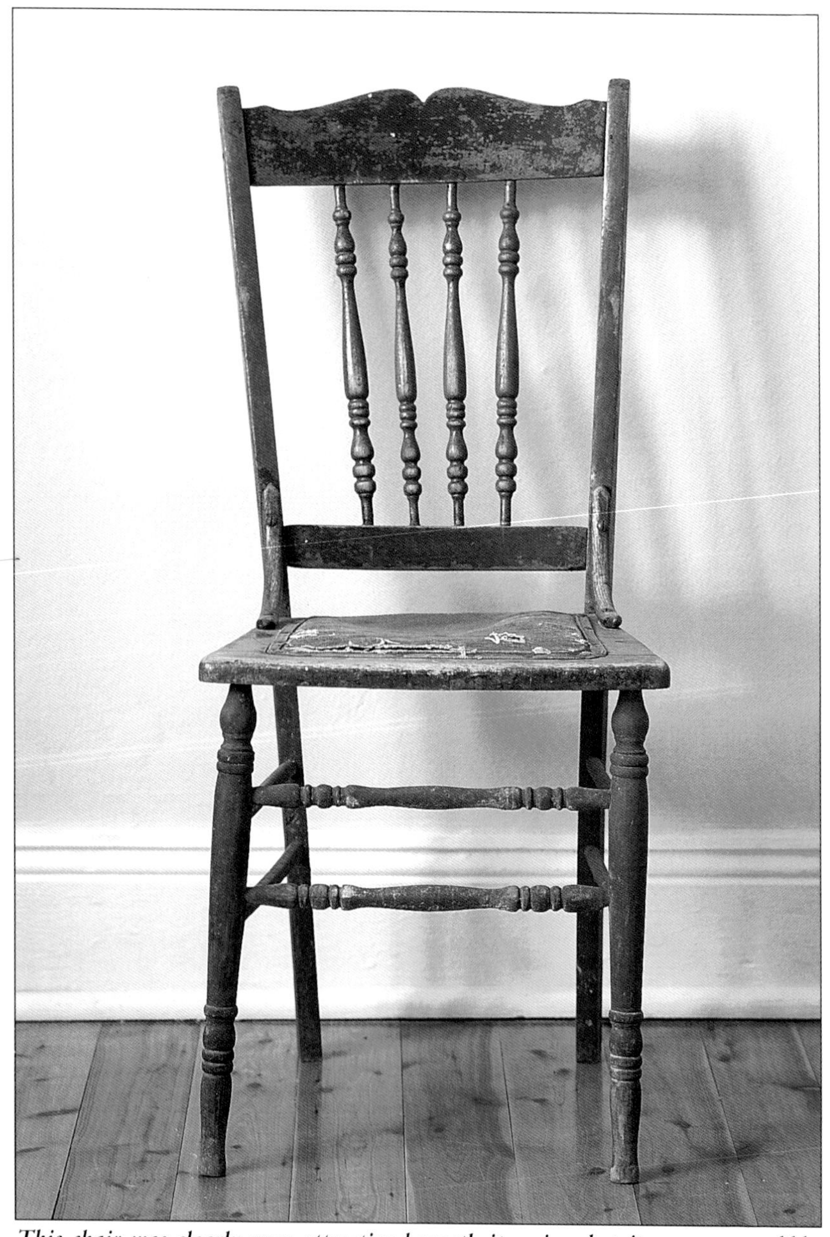

This chair was clearly very attractive beneath its grime but it was very wobbly and the seat needed replacing.

Repairing a chair

This kitchen chair was in a bad state of repair but its classic appearance and attractive turned legs made it worth repairing. The techniques used to repair it can be applied to many other types of furniture.

EQUIPMENT

- Pincers
- Hammer
- Chisel
- Nail punch
- Tape measure
- PVA adhesive
- Dowelling rod
- Bar or other clamp

The plywood base of the seat was broken and full of woodworm holes. It needed to be entirely replaced.

METHOD

1 Using pincers, hammer and chisel, remove the old seat. Work slowly and carefully to avoid damaging the surrounding wood.

2 Pull out any remaining nails. If the nails cannot be removed, punch them in below the surface.

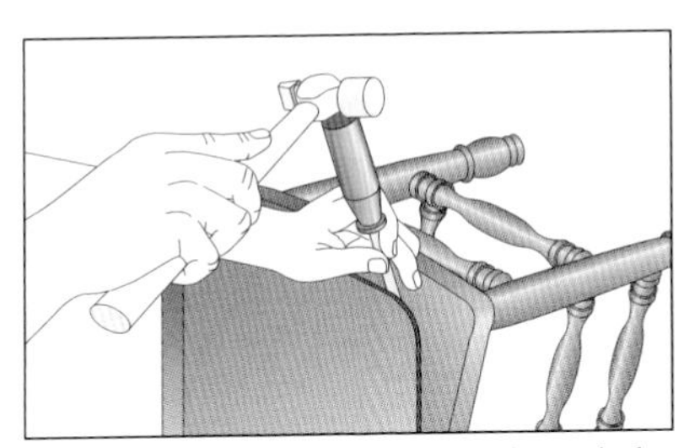

1 Use the hammer and chisel, and the pincers if necessary, to remove the old seat. Don't damage the wood.

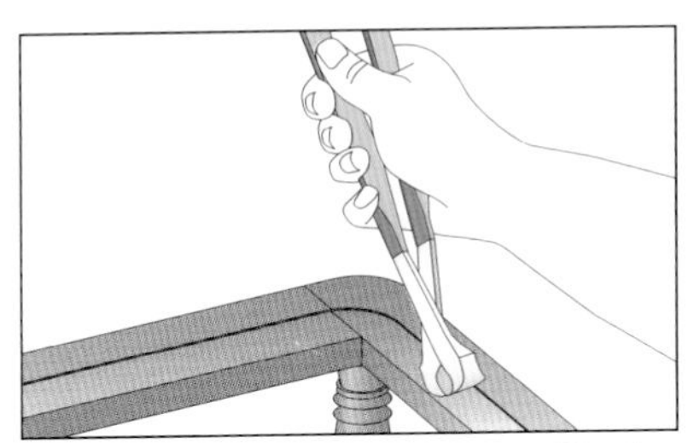

2 Use pincers to remove any old pins or nails. Punch in any that can not be pulled out.

PROFESSIONAL PAINT STRIPPERS

A lot of effort can be saved when stripping off old finishes, especially if the furniture pieces are large, by taking them to a professional paint stripper where the items are dipped into a large vat of hot caustic soda stripper. This process is very efficient but it is only suitable for solid timber pieces, not for furniture with a veneered finish or bentwood chairs. You will also need to be careful that all the stripper residue has been removed before you apply a new finish.

When the piece is returned, wash it down thoroughly with vinegar. Apply the vinegar liberally with a brush, working it into any cracks and hard-to-reach areas. The vinegar neutralises any left-over caustic solution, which can be seen as a white powder. If you can still see white powder after this treatment, apply a second vinegar wash to remove it all.

Allow the piece to dry thoroughly and sand it smooth before applying the new finish.

3 Check that the legs are secure. If the legs are loose, detach them (taking care not to damage the timber), labelling each leg clearly so that it can be replaced in the correct position. Scrape off any old adhesive and then apply adhesive to the socket and end of the leg. Press the leg firmly into the socket and clamp the chair together until the adhesive has thoroughly dried. Repeat the process for the other legs.

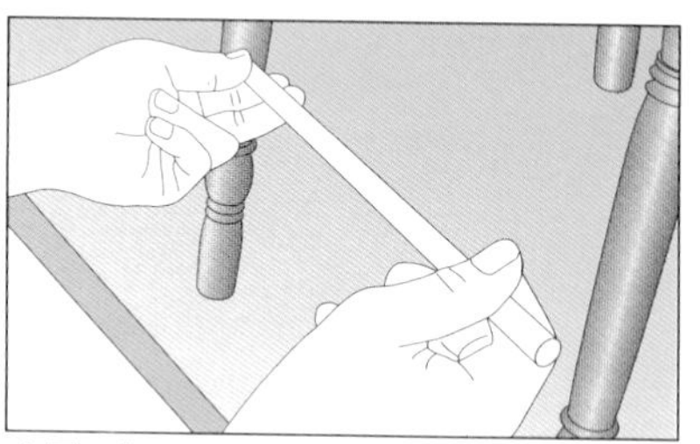

4 To fit a new rail, place the rail into one hole. Then work it into the other hole and centre it.

4 To fit a new rail between the legs, measure the distance between the legs, plus the depth of one hole (which the rail will fit into). Cut a piece of dowelling rod to this measurement. Put a small amount of adhesive into each hole, fit one end of the rail into one hole, work the other end into the other hole, then centre the rail and allow the adhesive to dry.

5 To replace the seat, make a template of the seat shape with paper and check that it fits in place. Use it to cut out the shape from plywood (about 9–12 mm (3/8–1/2 in) thick plywood is best). If desired, cut out the same shape in foam and glue it to the plywood. Cover the foam with thick calico, pulling it tight and stapling it to the bottom of the plywood. Re-cover with desired fabric.

Stripped of its old finish and with the legs and rails refitted, this chair is now ready for its new finish (see pages 32–3).

Simple repairs

REPAIRING DRAWER RAILS

Drawer rails may be broken away where the drawer locks penetrated into them, especially if the lock has ever been forced. It would be difficult to replace the rail but this problem can be easily fixed by inserting a small length of brass bar into the rail (see page 49).

1 Use a hacksaw to cut the brass long enough to cover any splitting. With a high speed steel (HSS) bit, drill a clearance hole at each end of the brass and countersink the holes.

2 Hold the brass bar against the rail and use a pencil to mark on the timber the area to be chiselled out. Using a tenon saw, make shallow cuts (to the thickness of the brass) in the marked area. Chisel out the marked area.

3 Clean and seal the brass (see box on page 31) and screw into place. Lacquer the screw heads.

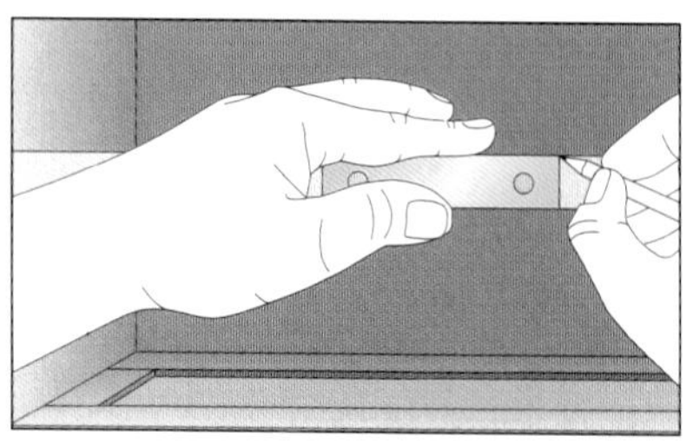

2 Hold the brass bar against the rail and use a pencil to mark on the timber the area to be chiselled out.

REPAIRING DRAWER RUNNERS

Drawer runners in old pieces of furniture are often worn away so that the drawers are difficult to pull out and push in. They are not very difficult to repair.

1 Use a chisel to pare away the worn timber of the runner until the runner is once again level.

2 Nail or glue a thin strip of hardwood to the runner to build it back to the required thickness.

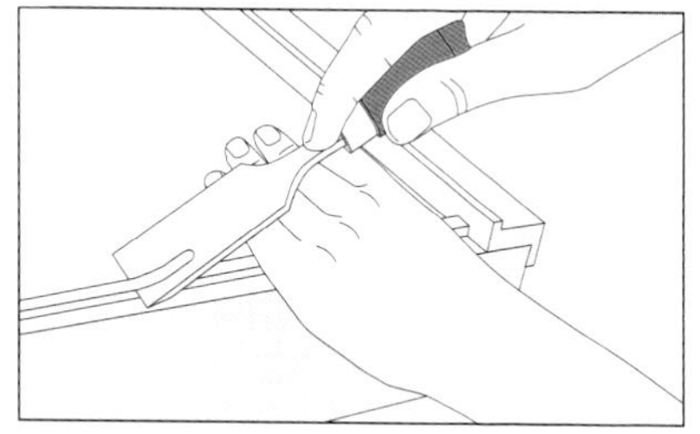

1 Chisel away the worn timber of the runner until the runner is once again level along its length.

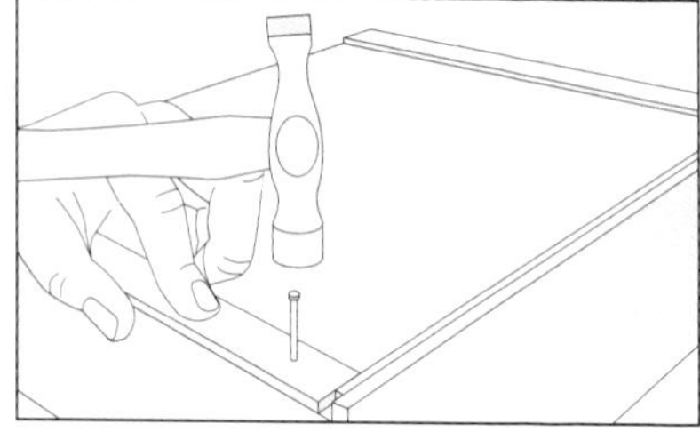

2 Nail a thin strip of hardwood to the levelled runner to return it to its original thickness.

FILLING GAPS AND HOLES

Gaps, holes and dents are one of the most common defects found in old furniture and they can ruin an otherwise attractive piece.

- Long, narrow gaps can be filled with a DIY filler, which can then be painted over.
- Cracks and splits in wood and holes, including nail and screw holes, can be filled with wood filler, using a putty knife. Choose one to match the timber. To get a good finish in difficult areas you might need to make two or even three applications, sanding lightly between to remove uneven surfaces. Sand with fine abrasive paper. If water-based wood filler is difficult to work with, add a little water.
- Missing corners or projections can be built up with plastic wood filler, or with shaped wood glued in place.
- Dents and hollows, where the wood has been compressed but not removed, can be dealt with by placing a thick, damp cloth over the area and then placing a hot domestic iron over it. The steam will raise the compacted wood.

Timber was shaped and glued to this broken corner (see page 17). Plastic wood could have been used instead.

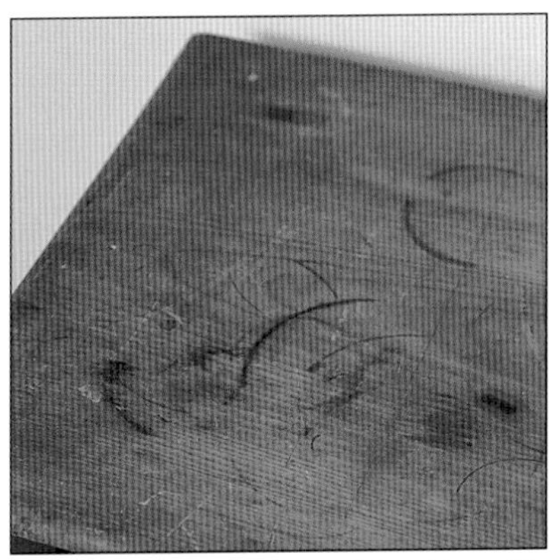

The scorch marks on this side table were unsightly. They were sanded out before the table was refinished.

REMOVING SCORCH MARKS

Fine furniture can be disfigured by scorch marks and cigarette burns. Depending on the extent of the damage, they can be dealt with in several ways.

- Superficial marks may be removed using an abrasive paste, such as a liquid metal polish, on a soft cloth.
- Most scorch marks need to be scraped or sanded out. If the burn is deep, the resulting hole can be filled with wood filler.

CLEANING BRASS

Clean brass handles or hinges with a brass brush or nylon scourer and then use brass polish. If desired, the brass can then be sealed by spraying with brass lacquer, which is available in spray cans. Use a small brush to apply it to screw heads.

The final touch for this repaired chair was a finish consisting of several coats of acrylic paint. It will now withstand normal wear and tear.

Using acrylic paints

Water-based acrylic paint is the paint most often used. It is easy to apply and the brushes are cleaned in water.

METHOD

1 Prepare the item for finishing (see box on page 53).

2 Apply the first layer of primer; leave to dry.

3 Use the filler and filling knife to fill any cracks or holes, which will show up now. Sand the flat areas of the chair with fine grade abrasive paper, and rub the legs and rails with the steel wool.

4 Dust off with the brush or soft cloth and apply a second layer of primer. Allow to dry.

5 Sand the flat areas with very fine abrasive paper, and the legs and rails with steel wool.

6 Apply the first layer of top coat. To avoid runs and pools of paint, feather out the wet paint with a drier brush, particularly on the more ornate areas. Leave to dry.

7 Sand the flat areas with very fine abrasive paper, and the legs and rails with steel wool. Dust off with the soft brush or cloth, then clean carefully with the tack cloth before applying the final layer of top coat. Leave to dry.

EQUIPMENT

- Primer/undercoat
- Paint brushes
- Wood filler
- Filling knife
- Abrasive paper: one sheet each of fine and very fine grade
- Steel wool or nylon scourer
- Soft brush or cloth
- Top coat
- Tack cloth

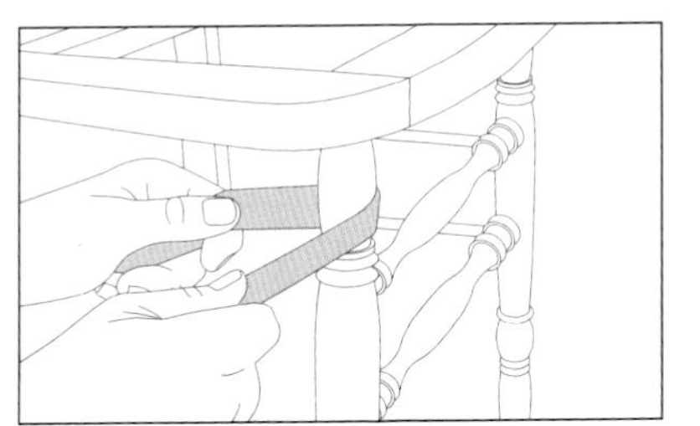

3 Use steel wool to sand back the undercoat on rounded parts such as rails and legs.

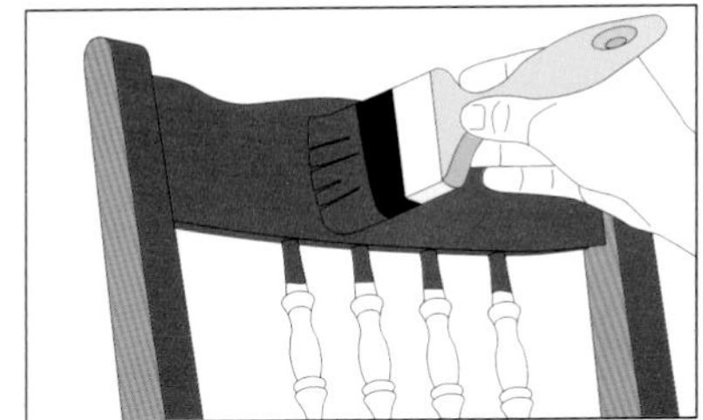

6 Apply the first layer of top coat, feathering out any runs and pools with a dryish brush. Leave to dry.

Using solvent-based paints

Solvent-based paint is now less popular than acrylic (water-based) paint as it has a longer drying time and the brushes must be cleaned in white spirit. However, it does have better wearing qualities and so a gloss version was ideal for this child's desk, which could be expected to suffer lots of wear and tear.

METHOD

1 Prepare the item for finishing (see the box on page 53). Apply one coat of primer all over the piece, and leave it to dry.

2 Using the abrasive paper, sand over the primer lightly. Do not rub through to the bare wood. If there are places where you accidentally rubbed through the primer, you will need to touch up those areas before adding the top coat. Wipe clean with a rag.

3 Apply the appropriate colour of undercoat. For the best finish, work with long brush strokes, using the tip of the bristles and a light pressure. Leave the paint to dry.

EQUIPMENT

- Primer and undercoat
- Paint brush
- Abrasive paper: two sheets of very fine grade
- Solvent-based gloss top coat
- Clean rag
- White spirit (for cleaning brushes)

4 Using the very fine abrasive paper, sand over the item lightly. Be careful not to rub through the undercoat to the primer. Wipe the piece clean with a rag.

5 Apply the gloss top coat but do not sand it back. The finish will be smooth and glossy.

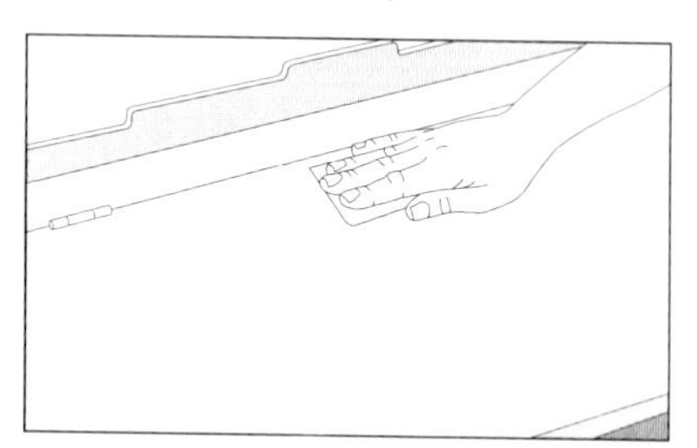

2 Sand lightly over the primer, using the abrasive paper, long strokes and a light, even pressure.

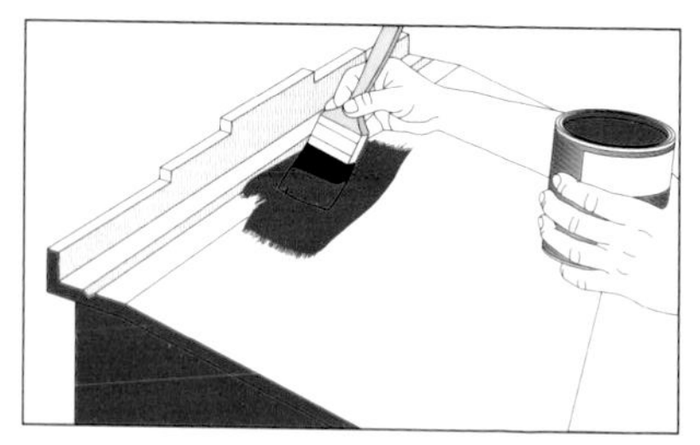

3 Apply the top coat, using long brush strokes and the tips of the bristles only.

Gloss solvent-based paint gives an attractive, hard-wearing finish to this desk.

The beading around the doors and edges of this kitchen cupboard were picked out in red, providing a striking contrast with the green of the flat areas.

Painting using two colours

Very effective results can be obtained by using two or more contrasting colours when painting a piece of furniture. The method is the same as one-colour painting but the areas need to be carefully masked so that the edges are neat.

EQUIPMENT

- Primer/undercoat
- Paint brushes
- Abrasive paper: two sheets of very fine grade
- Cork block
- Soft brush or cloth
- Tack cloth
- Nylon scourer
- Top coat (main colour)
- Contrasting top coat
- Low tack masking tape or fine line tape (waterproof)*

* Available from car accessory shops

METHOD

1 Prepare the item for finishing (see the box on page 53).

2 Paint the entire item with primer, including any doors and beading. It is important to brush the paint into the grain, working it in to seal the wood. Leave the piece until the paint is completely dry.

3 Sand lightly with the abrasive paper, being very careful not to rub the primer away and expose bare wood. This will happen very easily on corners, so go gently. (If you do rub back to bare wood, touch it up before you do the first top coat.) You can use a block, but you'll get a better feel using half a sheet of abrasive paper folded into thirds. Dust with a soft brush or cloth, and then with a tack cloth for a completely dust-free surface.

4 Apply the first top coat for the main colour (here it is green). Work the paint in well and use long, light strokes to finish. Leave to dry.

5 Sand lightly using abrasive paper; once again be very careful on the corners. A nylon scourer can be good for any rounded edges. Dust off with a soft brush or cloth, and then a tack cloth. Apply a second top coat.

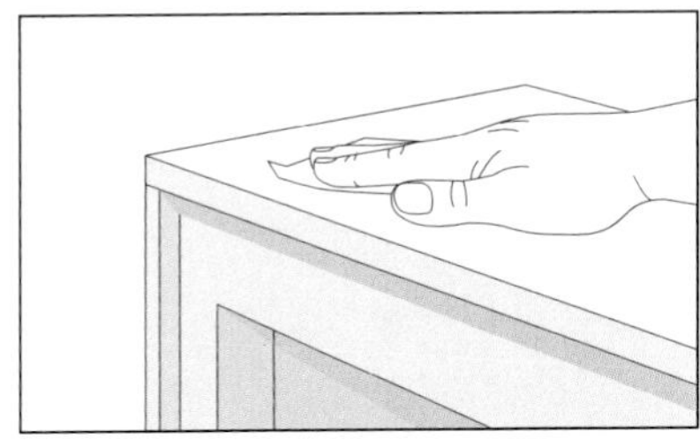

5 Lightly sand over the first top coat, being very careful not to sand through the paint especially on the corners.

REPLACING HINGES

The hinges on the cupboard were replaced with piano hinges. These are some of the easiest hinges to fit.

1 Plane along the side where the hinges were housed, to make a flush surface.

2 With a hacksaw, cut the piano hinge to length, about 4 mm (5/32 in) shorter than the door height. Open the hinge wide and place it on the door with the back (barrel) of the hinge sitting proud of the face.

3 Fasten the hinge with No. 4 gauge 5/8 inch brass screws. The piano hinge is fitted before the item is painted. It can be removed again before painting.

1 Plane away the housings from the old hinges to make a flush surface.

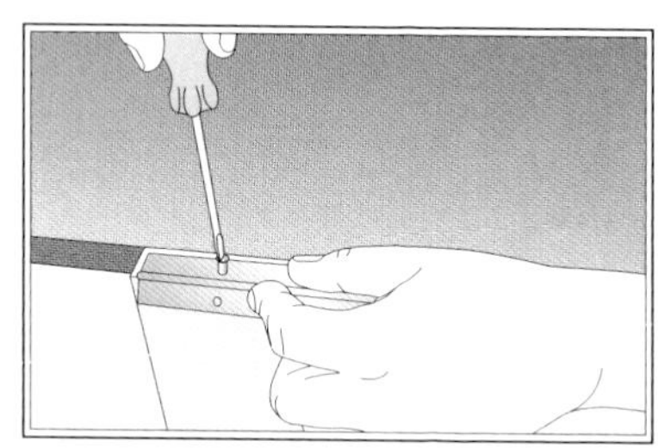

3 Fasten the hinge in place using as many No.4 gauge 5/8 inch brass screws as are necessary.

6 Allow the last top coat to dry completely to minimise the chance of it being damaged when the tape is pulled off. Apply tape around the edges of the area to receive the contrasting colour. Use only low tack masking tape so the finish won't be damaged. Push the tape down firmly, so contrasting paint won't run under the edge.

7 Lightly sand the area to be painted with abrasive paper and remove dust with a tack cloth.

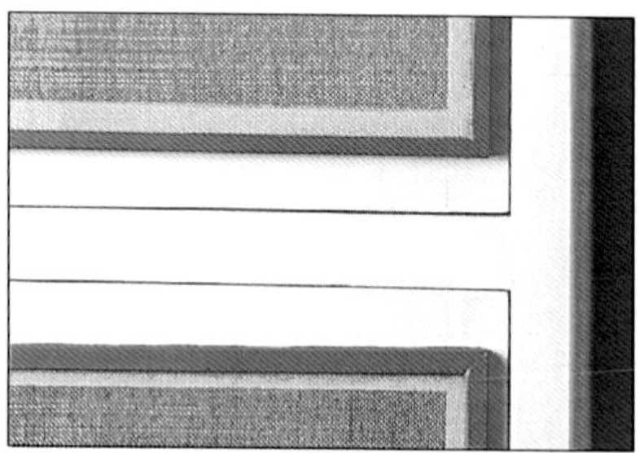

Careful masking is essential to produce a result like this.

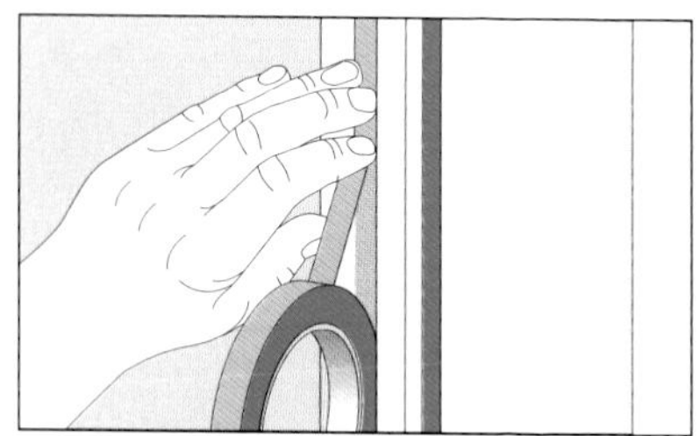

6 Apply tape around the area to be painted with the second, contrasting colour. Push the tape down firmly.

REPLACING METAL SCREEN

1 Before painting or adding any other finish, remove the old metal gauze by lifting the beading from the doors with a chisel and working from the inside edge, so that any marks you make will be covered by the new gauze.

2 Cut the new gauze to the correct size and fix it to the door using either a heavy stapler, staple gun or small flat-head nails. Place the beads over the staples/nails and fasten them down with panel pins punched below the surface.

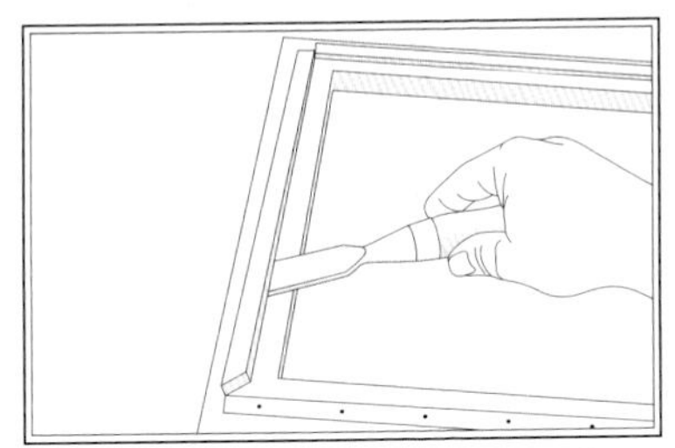

1 Remove beading from the doors with a chisel. Work from the inside edge so that marks on the timber will be covered by the new gauze.

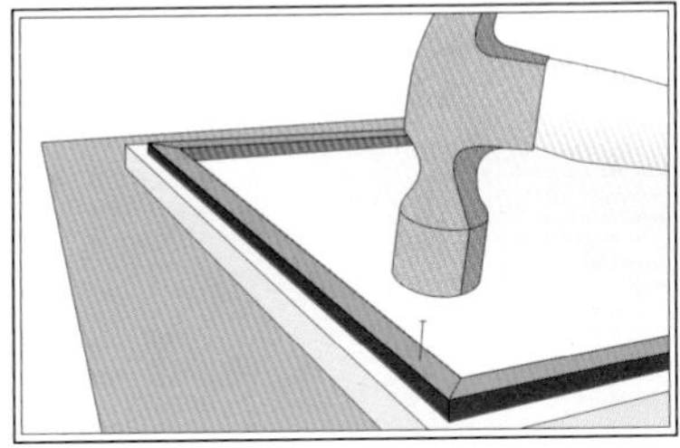

2 Fasten the new gauze to the door with staples or nails and place beads over them. Fasten the beads down with panel pins.

8 Paint the masked-off area with the contrasting paint. Sand lightly using abrasive paper or a nylon scourer. Use the tack cloth to remove any dust. Apply the second top coat of paint in the same way and then leave it to dry thoroughly.

9 Remove the masking tape slowly, a little at a time, making sure no paint is being pulled off. If any paint starts to lift, change the direction and angle at which you are removing the tape. This is the crucial step, so take your time.

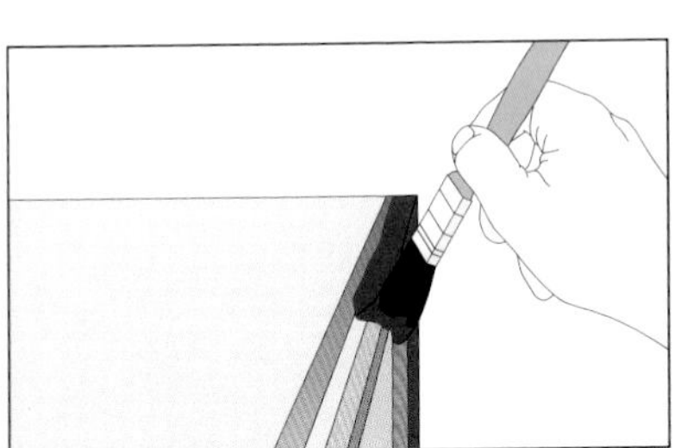

8 Carefully apply contrasting top coat within the masked-off area. Sand back and apply a second coat.

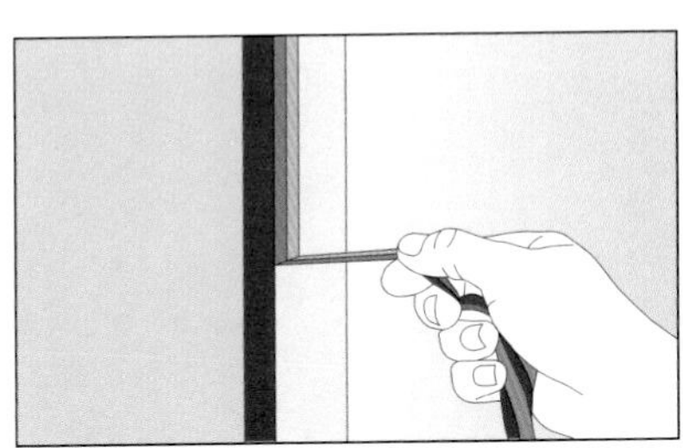

9 Remove the tape slowly. If any paint starts to lift, change the angle at which you're pulling.

Applying a paint wash and beeswax

The soft finish on this dresser was achieved with a paint wash and wax. Painting furniture such as this involves some preparation if the result is to look professional, as it has to be disassembled and attention paid to masking.

METHOD

1 Prepare the item for finishing (see the box on page 53).

2 Dilute the paint with an equal amount of water, mixing until they are well combined. The proportions can be changed if you want a deeper or lighter colour.

3 Work on only a small area (such as a door or a side) at a time so that you can rub off the paint before it dries. Brush on a generous layer of paint and use a clean rag to wipe off excess paint. To achieve an even finish, wipe firmly and use long, continuous strokes. As soon as the rag is wet with paint, turn to a clean part or change rags. If the paint dries before you can wipe it off, apply another coat and wipe it off immediately (and in future work in smaller areas). Leave it to dry.

4 Using a clean rag, apply beeswax in a rubbing motion, to fill the grain. Allow it to dry for about 20 minutes, and then rub the surface briskly with a soft cloth. This will take off any excess wax and buff the surface to a soft sheen. Leave it for 30 minutes and then repeat the waxing. The more coats, the better the finish.

EQUIPMENT

- Acrylic paint
- Rubber gloves
- Paint brush
- Clean rags
- Beeswax

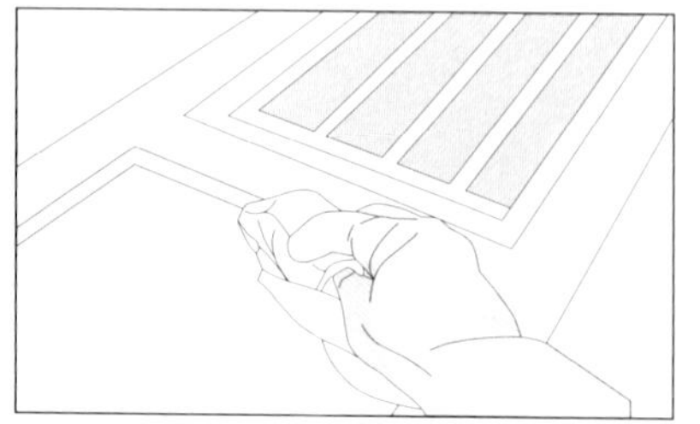

3 Brush on the paint and then wipe off excess paint with a clean rag, using long, firm strokes.

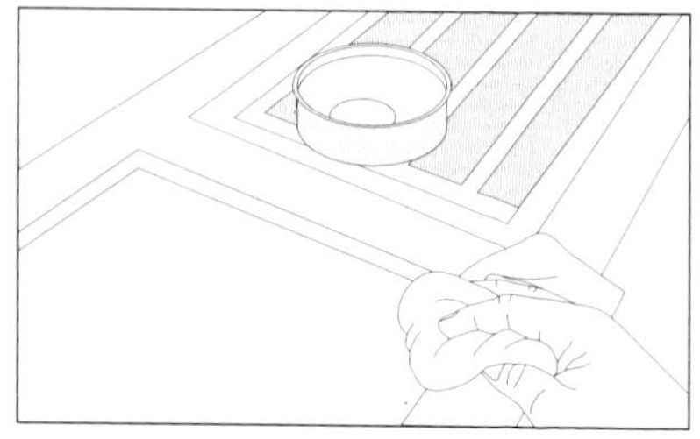

4 Use a clean rag to rub beeswax into the surface. The more coats of wax you use, the better the finish.

The soft colour of the paint wash makes a perfect background for the coloured glass in this old-fashioned dresser. The smooth finish was achieved by rubbing beeswax into the surface.

Spray painting is the most efficient way to paint metal furniture such as this bedhead, as it allows even coverage of the decorated areas as well as the tubular sections.

Spray painting metal

Metal can be painted with a brush but the most even coverage is achieved by spray painting, especially the decorative areas. Traditionally a spray-gun was used but aerosol cans are now commonly available and they are less messy to use. Make sure you choose a paint suitable for metal.

METHOD

1 Take the tack rag and wipe over the item to remove any dust. If you can see any rust, apply a coat of rust converter.

2 Hold the can of primer about 15 cm (6 in) away and spray on a fine, even coating. Leave it to dry, and then spray on a second fine coat. This is better than one heavy coat, which may run. Leave it to dry.

3 Using the scourer, lightly rub the surface, making sure you do not rub through the primer to bare metal. If you do rub through the primer, touch up those areas before adding the top coat. Wipe over with the tack rag to remove any dust.

EQUIPMENT

- Tack rag
- Zinc-based, rust-inhibiting primer (spray paint)
- Nylon scourer
- Top coat (spray paint suitable for metal)

4 Holding the can of top coat about 15 cm (6 in) away, again spray on a fine, even coat. Leave it to dry, rub lightly with the scourer and then wipe with a tack rag. Spray on a second coat of paint to finish.

HINT

When spray painting, always work in a well-lit, dust-free area.

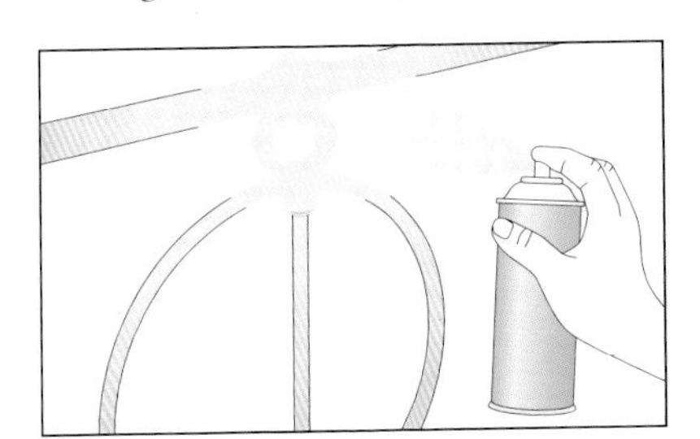

2 Hold the can of primer about 15 cm (6 in) from the furniture and give a fine, even coating to surfaces.

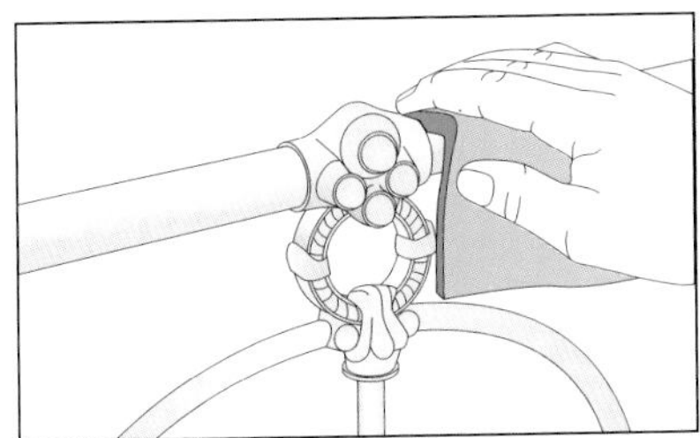

3 Lightly rub the surface with the scourer, being careful not to rub through the primer.

Spray painting cane

Spray painting is the most successful way to give an old piece of cane furniture a new lease of life. The process is quick and simple. For a natural look, substitute polyurethane varnish.

EQUIPMENT

- Spray undercoat (three cans were needed for this chair)
- Abrasive paper, fine grade
- Soft brush or cloth
- Spray top coat (six cans were used on this chair)
- Trimming knife
- Tack cloth

METHOD

1 Make sure the item is dust free and prepared for finishing (see the box on page 53). Place it on old newspapers and ensure that the surrounding area is covered.

2 Spray the chair with undercoat, holding the can about 15 cm (6 in) away from the surface. Allow the paint to dry thoroughly.

3 Using abrasive paper, rub back the entire item. Dust it off with a soft brush or cloth.

4 Spray on the first top coat and allow it to dry. Rub it back with abrasive paper. Use a trimming knife to cut off wispy bits of cane.

5 Use a tack cloth to make sure the chair is dust free, and then spray on a second top coat.

PAINT RUNS

When painting, keep your eyes open for any runs and try to brush them out before the paint dries. If you miss any, sand them out and re-paint the area. Cut off bad runs with a sharp blade or chisel. This is easier while the paint is still soft.

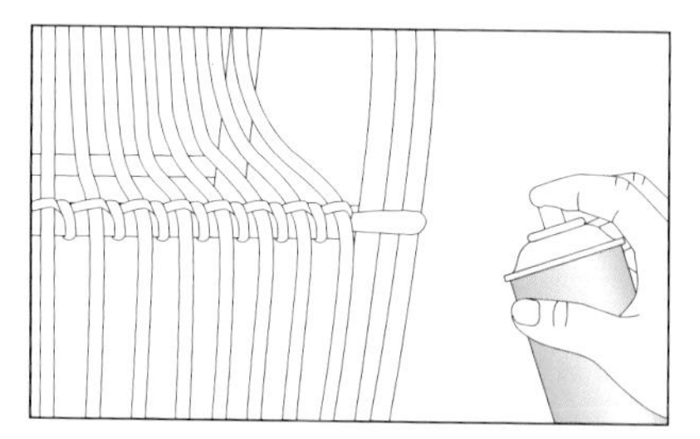

2 Spray on the undercoat, holding the can 15 cm (6 in) away from the surface to achieve a fine, even coat.

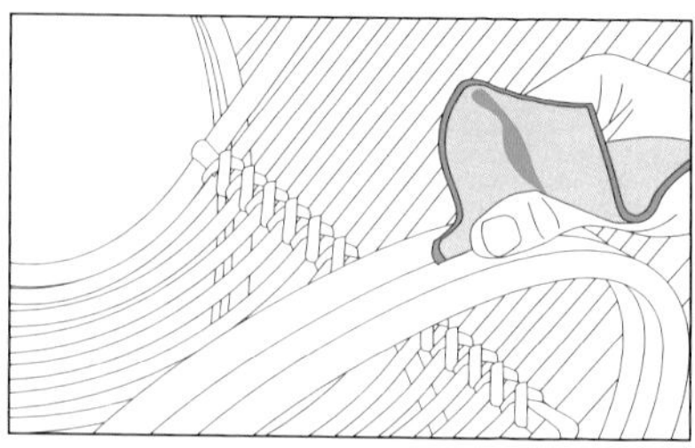

3 Use abrasive paper to rub back the undercoat. Remove any dust with a soft brush.

Properly undercoated and given a beautiful top coat, this cane chair will grace your conservatory or patio for years to come.

The beautiful grain of the timber on this chest of drawers is shown to perfection by the simple waxed finish.

Applying wax finishes

Wax gives a soft sheen to furniture while preserving its natural appearance. The surface is, however, easily marked unless it has been sealed with a clear varnish before waxing.

METHOD

1 Prepare the item for finishing (see the box on page 53).

2 Apply wax to the item with a fine steel wool pad or nylon scourer, making sure to rub it well into the grain. Try not to leave any build up of wax on the surface.

3 Within a couple of minutes use the lint-free cloth to rub the area that has just been waxed to even out the coating. The surface will feel sticky, but keep rubbing and change to a clean part of the cloth whenever it gets clogged. Continue rubbing firmly as long as possible as this will polish the surface. Hold the furniture firmly while you polish, grasping it through a clean cloth. This will prevent grease from your hand transferring to the timber.

4 Repeat this process at least once more. Extra coats of wax will enhance the finish.

EQUIPMENT

- Furniture wax
- Steel wool pad or nylon scourer
- Lint-free cloth
- Clean cloth

CLEANING A WAXED SURFACE

Badly marked pieces can be rubbed with a nylon scourer, but always rub in the direction of the wood grain. Otherwise, wipe with a cloth dampened in warm, soapy water and dry with a clean, absorbent cloth.

2 Apply the wax to the furniture with fine steel wool or a nylon scourer. Be sure to rub with the grain.

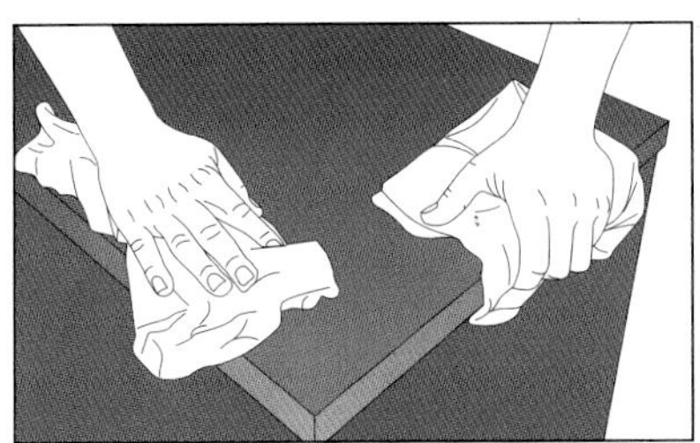

3 Hold the piece firmly with a clean cloth in one hand while polishing with the other hand.

Applying varnish

Varnish is a clear finish that coats the surface of the timber. Most varnishes today are polyurethane, solvent-based varnishes and come in matt, gloss or 'satin' (low gloss) finish. Coloured varnishes are also available. Varnishes will resist heat and staining.

METHOD

1 Prepare the item for finishing (see the box on page 53). Just before varnishing, wipe the item thoroughly with the tack cloth to remove any remaining dust, paying particular attention to grooves and details.

EQUIPMENT

- Polyurethane gloss varnish
- Paint brush
- Abrasive paper: two sheets of very fine grade
- Cork sanding block
- Nylon scourer
- Soft brush or cloth
- Tack cloth
- White spirit (for cleaning brushes)

2 Using a paint brush, apply the first coat of varnish. Take the varnish right around the lip of drawers or doors when you come to the edges. Leave to dry (this could take 1–3 days depending on the weather). The varnish should be completely hard before you proceed.

3 Sand the entire piece with abrasive paper around a cork block or folded sandpaper (don't use an orbital sander as it will cut through the varnish). Use a nylon scourer on corners and edges. Then dust off with a soft brush or cloth.

4 Repeat steps 2 and 3, using more abrasive paper. Clean off completely with a tack rag. Apply the third and final coat. Leave to dry.

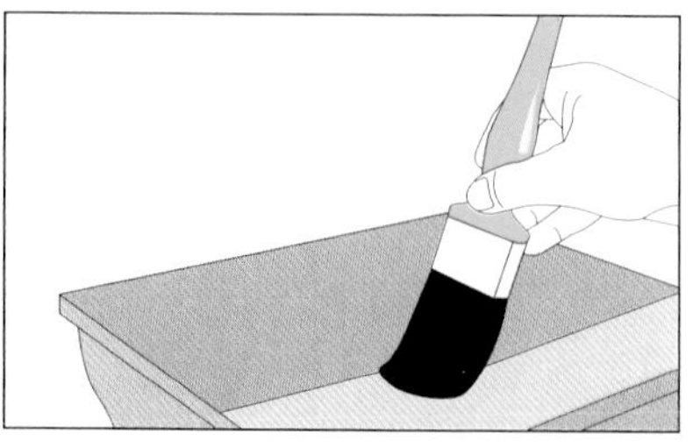

2 Apply the varnish with a paint brush. Leave it to dry for up to three days, until it is completely hard.

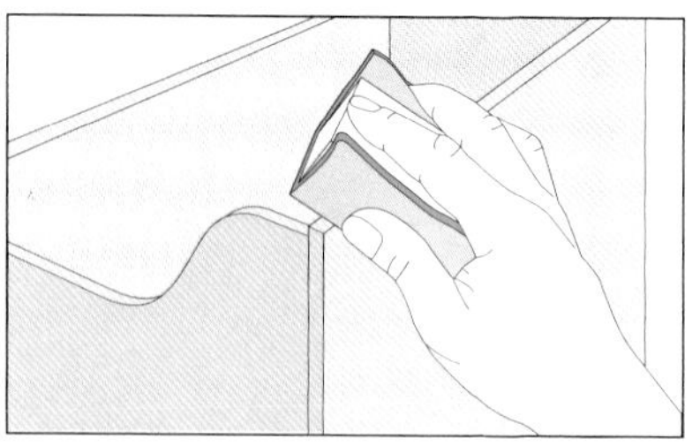

3 Sand over the entire item, using a nylon scourer on corners and edges to avoid removing the varnish.

This old wooden filing cabinet achieves a certain elegance when given a new varnished finish. The broken rails were repaired with brass strips (see page 30).

This plain towel rack has been revitalised by the application of a teak-coloured varnish. For a more traditional look you could use a darker finish.

Applying coloured varnish

Coloured varnish has been tinted with a stain so that it changes the colour of the timber. It is available in various colours and gives a quicker result than the traditional method of staining the item and then adding a clear varnish. However, it can be a little tricky to get an even colour.

EQUIPMENT

- Tack cloth
- Water-based coloured varnish
- Paint brush
- Abrasive paper: very fine
- Nylon scourer
- Soft brush or cloth

METHOD

1 Prepare the item for finishing (see the box on page 53). Just before you begin varnishing, wipe over the item thoroughly with the tack cloth to remove any remaining dust. Pay particular attention to grooves and details where dust settles. If any dust remains it will be visible in the varnished surface.

2 Apply the coloured varnish with a paint brush. It is important to brush with the grain (rather than across) at all times to avoid uneven marks. Before you wash your brush out in water, look carefully over the whole piece for any runs or drips, as they are a lot easier to brush out now than to try and sand off later.

CLEANING PAINTED OR VARNISHED SURFACES

To clean painted and varnished surfaces, dip a clean cloth into soapy water and wring it out. Use it to wipe over the surface. Then give the surface a second wipe with a clean cloth dampened with water only. Leave to dry.

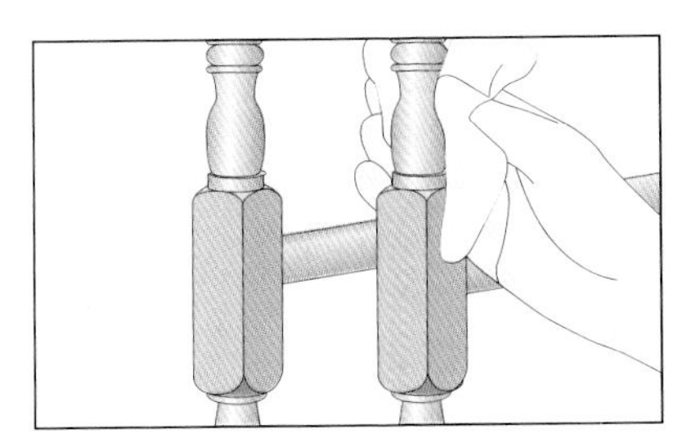

1 Wipe over the item with a tack cloth to make sure there is no dust on the surface.

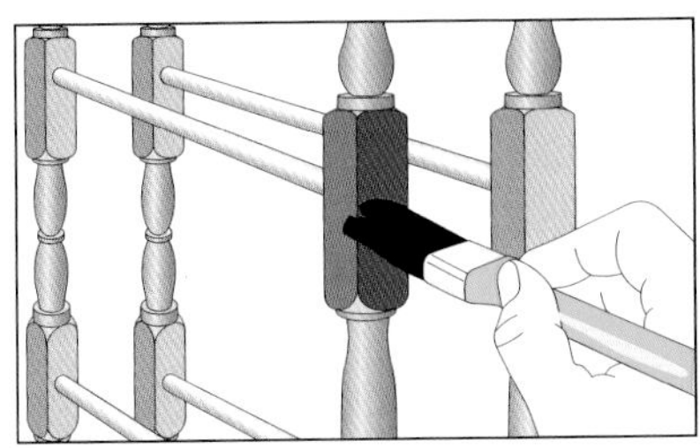

2 Apply the coloured varnish with a brush, brushing with the wood grain to avoid brush marks.

Coloured varnish was applied after the item was thoroughly cleaned.

3 Leave the varnish to dry: it may take a little longer than the time recommended by the manufacturer but the varnish must be dry and hard, or sanding could damage the finish. Using very fine abrasive paper, sand all the easy areas, being very careful not to rub through the varnish, especially on the edges. On more ornate areas, use the nylon scourer, as it is less aggressive. Dust off with a soft brush or cloth.

4 Repeat steps 2 and 3 to give a second and final coat of varnish.

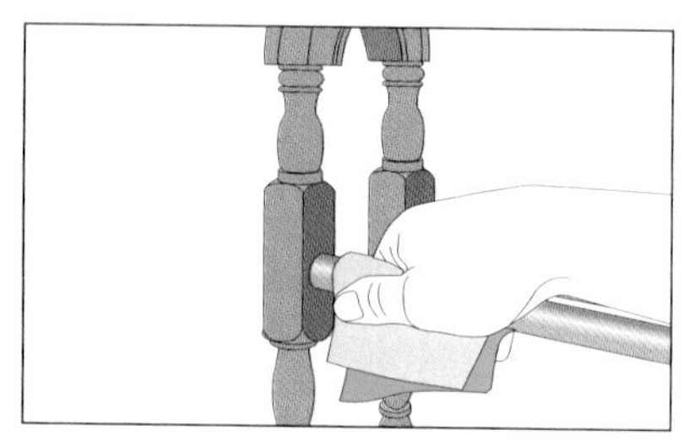

3 Sand back the varnish. In ornate or round areas use the stripping pad as it is less likely to damage the finish.

VARNISHING HINTS

- Always work in a well-ventilated area when applying solvent-based varnishes.
- Use only brushes in good condition as bristles that come out and get caught in the varnished surface can ruin your work.
- Before you begin work, test coloured varnishes on the underside of the piece to be certain you will end up with the colour you want.
- If you have achieved the required colour and the piece needs another coat of varnish, use a clear varnish.
- Coloured varnishes can sometimes be darkened by adding spirit-based stains.
- The colour of varnishes can be diluted using water or white spirit (check the manufacturer's instructions on the container).
- Pine is usually treated with a clear varnish, which gives it the rich, golden colour that is currently so popular.
- If furniture is to be used in the bathroom or other damp area, make sure you coat underneath the feet or base so that the timber is completely sealed.
- If you want a really smooth finished surface, use fine steel wool to rub a coat of beeswax into the varnish, but be sure to wait until the varnish is completely dry.

PREPARING FOR FINISHING

Whether your item has been freshly stripped or sitting around for some time, it will need attention before you apply a finish. This is especially so for transparent finishes such as varnishes and French polish but a little attention helps any finish adhere better.

1 Ensure the piece of furniture is quite clean. To remove dirt and grease, wash with sugar soap, warm water and a nylon scourer. Rinse it clean and let it dry completely. This also raises any loose grain.

2 Remove doors, drawers, hinges and handles. Punch in protruding nails. Cover glass panels with newspaper, attaching it at the edges with masking tape. Ensure the tape is flush with edges and corners.

3 Sand with medium grade abrasive paper, sanding with the grain as much as possible to remove any raised grain. Sand large areas with an orbital sander, smaller areas with a cork block and abrasive paper, and grooves with folded abrasive paper. Make sure you round all sharp corners as this helps the finish go around the corners.

4 Fill cracks or holes with wood filler, smoothing the surface with a putty knife. Leave it to dry, then sand with fine grade abrasive paper. Wipe the whole item with a tack cloth to remove any dust.

5 Change to a finer grade abrasive paper and sand again. Wipe with a tack cloth to remove any dust.

6 Stain any parts of the item that don't match (see step 2 on page 60).

7 Use a small paint brush to apply rust converter to screw heads or nails that are showing.

8 Give a final wipe over with a clean rag to remove any dust.

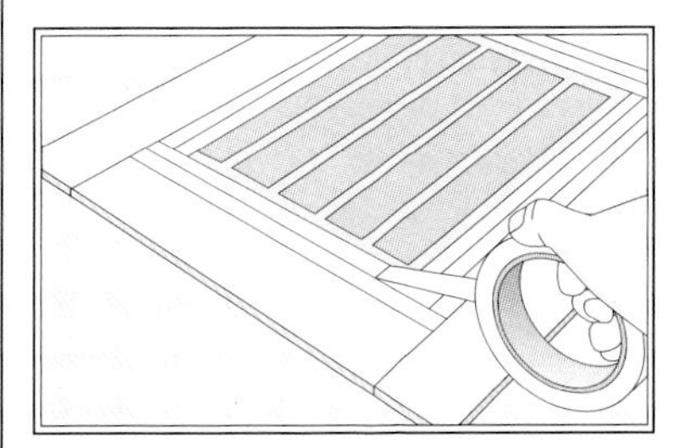

2 Cover glass panels or areas you won't be painting with newspaper, attaching it with masking tape.

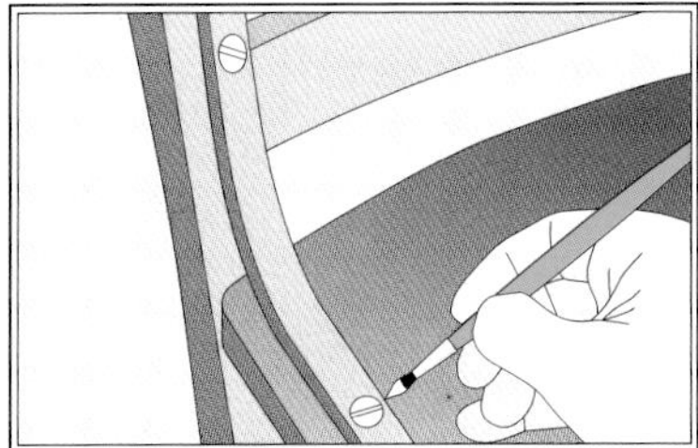

7 Treat any screw heads that are showing with rust converter, using a small brush.

Applying French polish

French polish is made by dissolving shellac in alcohol. It gives a beautiful, fine, glossy finish but it is not easy to apply. It is easily marked and stained.

METHOD

1 Prepare the item for finishing (see the box on page 53).

2 Wearing gloves, apply French polish to small areas (such as the legs of this table) with a small paint brush, and use a small applicator (see the box on page 57) to remove excess polish and even out the finish, going with the grain where possible. Work on a small area at a time, as the polish dries quickly. If it feels sticky, it means you are working too slowly or on too large an area. The applicator can be re-wet with polish to work out the sticky area, but it is best to avoid this problem in the first place. The correct motion is to start with small circles, working into a figure eight movement and then long strokes with the grain (as shown in the diagram on page 56). Keep the applicator moving at all times, and when taking it off the surface 'slide' it off rather than abruptly lifting it. The pressure should be firm, but not hard enough to lift previous coats.

EQUIPMENT

- Gloves
- French polish
- Small paint brush
- Sheet cottonwool
- Soft lint-free cotton cloth
- Rubber band or string
- Shallow container
- Nylon scourer
- Abrasive paper: very fine grade
- Soft brush or cloth
- Tack cloth

3 For larger areas such as the table top, use a larger applicator to put the polish

2 Apply French polish to small areas with a small paint brush and use a small applicator to rub it in.

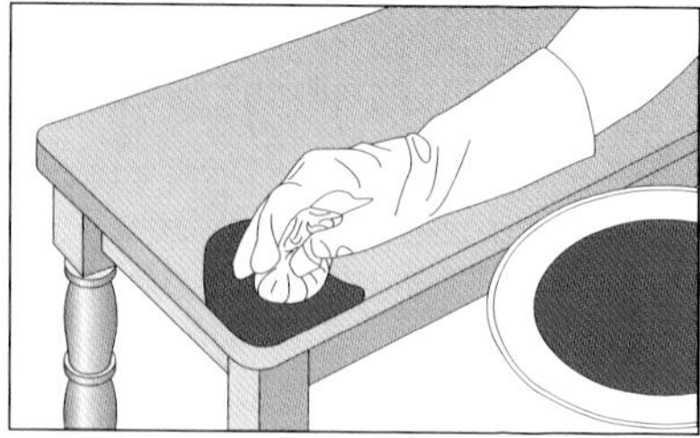

3 On large areas apply French polish with a larger applicator, dipping it into a shallow container of polish.

French polish is the finest of all polished finishes and can be well worth the extra care necessary for its application and maintenance.

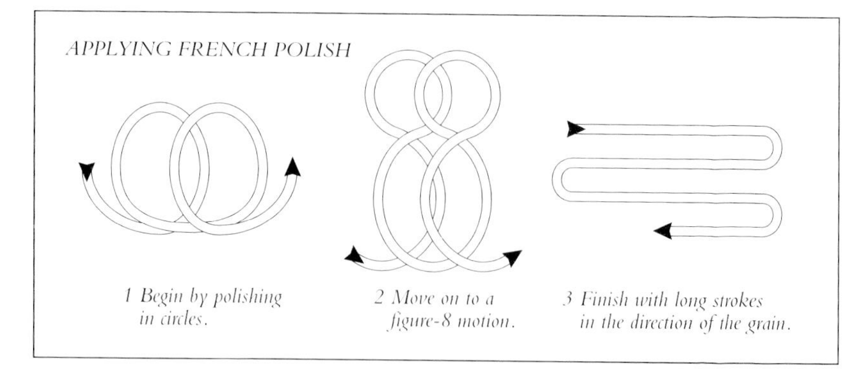

on, continually dipping the applicator into a shallow container of French polish. Work as described in step 2.

4 Use the nylon scourer to lightly rub the entire surface. Any drips or runs can be lightly sanded out with very fine abrasive paper. Dust off with a soft brush or cloth, and clean with the tack cloth.

5 Repeat the layers of French polish, using the scourer between each coat. We applied six coats of French polish to this table. Four coats would be the minimum for an acceptable finish. More than six will add to the depth of finish.

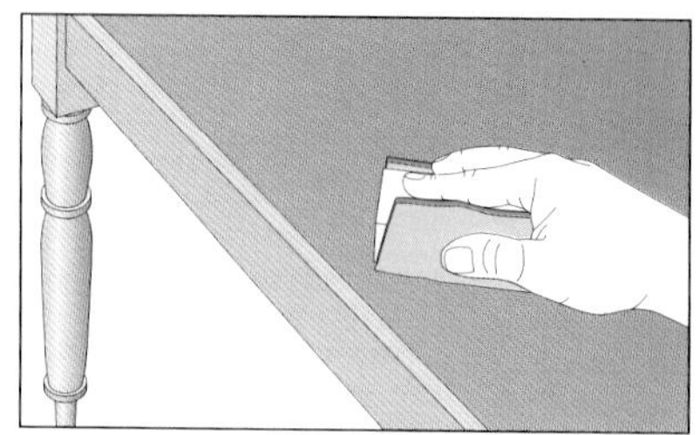

4 Lightly rub the surface with a nylon scourer and then sand out any runs with fine abrasive paper.

REPAIRING DAMAGE TO FRENCH POLISH

- If a French polished finish is scratched or chipped, there is no quick way to repair it. It should be sanded back or stripped with methylated spirits, and re-coated.
- Greasy or sticky marks can be wiped off the surface with a damp cloth. The surface should then be wiped dry immediately.
- To revive French polish first wash it with warm water and soap flakes. When it is thoroughly dry, apply a reviver of five parts white spirit, two parts linseed oil and one part turpentine, or use a proprietary reviver.
- If the surface has been exposed to sunlight it may be faded and the timber beneath bleached. Strip off the French polish (see pages 22–5), wash with diluted vinegar and when dry rub in a mixture of equal parts linseed oil and turpentine to revive the colour of the wood. Then reapply French polish.

MAKING A FRENCH POLISH APPLICATOR

The first step in creating a successful French polished surface is to make a proper applicator. A French polish applicator can be made in various sizes, depending on the size of the area you'll be working on. For a large applicator, start with a sheet of cottonwool about 200 mm (8 in) square; for a small one a sheet about 50 mm (2 in) square will be sufficient.

1 Take a piece of sheet cottonwool and fold it to form a flat, pear-shaped pad, smooth on one side (the 'top') and gathered together underneath. The pad should be firmly packed.

2 Drape a piece of soft, lint-free cotton cloth (a piece of old sheet is ideal) over the top of the pad, and twist it under the narrow end to form a firmly packed point. Gather the remaining cloth underneath the pad, patting the top of the pad firmly to flatten it out.

3 Tie off the cloth with string or secure it with a rubber band. There should be no gathers or wrinkles on the top, which will be used for rubbing the furniture. Any wrinkles in the cloth will result in uneven application of the polish and so streaky marks on the final polished surface.

4 Just before using the applicator the first time, undo the string and pour French polish into the cottonwool until it is wet but not dripping. Replace the string.

5 Press the applicator on a piece of clean paper to squeeze out any excess polish. You are now ready to begin work.

To store the applicator between coats, place it in an airtight container with about 10 mm (1/2 in) of methylated spirits in the bottom. This will prevent it drying out before you need it again.

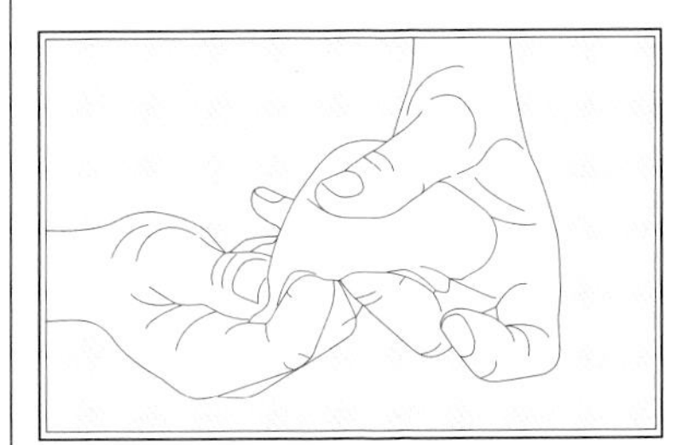

1 Fold a piece of cottonwool sheet to form a pear-like shape, flat on top and gathered underneath.

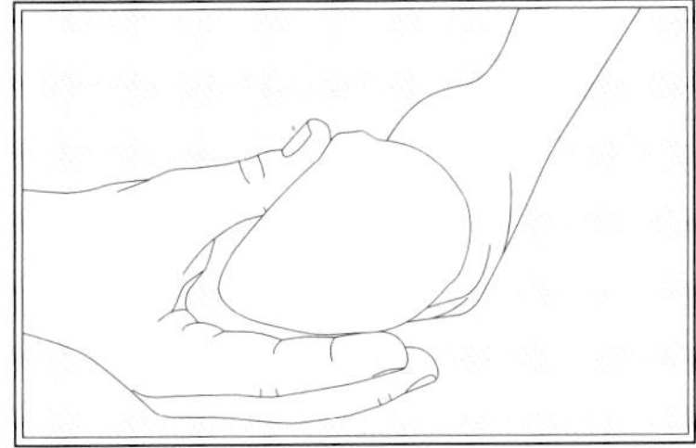

2 Drape a piece of soft, lint-free cotton cloth over the top of the cottonwool and twist it underneath.

This miniature chest of drawers was perfectly suited to the rather elaborate black lacquered finish.

Applying black lacquered finish

Lacquered finishes can be difficult for the non-professional to apply but "ebonizing" gives a finish that gives a similar result and yet is within the capability of most DIY enthusiasts.

METHOD

1 Prepare the item for finishing (see the box on page 53).

2 When applying the stain, make sure everything you need is close to hand, as it will dry quickly. Have a few rags handy. Wearing rubber gloves, apply a liberal coating of stain to one area at a time, with a medium brush. Before it has time to dry, wipe off any excess with a clean rag. Leave to dry and sand lightly.

3 To seal the stain, apply a coat of French polish. This can be done using the same method as was used to apply the stain. Brush it on, one area at a time, and remove the excess with a lint-free cloth.

4 After the French polish has dried, give the piece a very light sanding with a nylon scourer (use it over a cork block when working on the flat surfaces). Dust off with a soft brush or cloth.

5 Using a tack cloth, wipe all surfaces free of dust. As soon as the cloth gets filled with dust, turn it over to a clean surface.

6 Give the can of spray varnish a very thorough shaking. Spray two light coats within two hours of each other. Hold the can about 15–20 cm (6–8 in) away from the surface as this will prevent any runs.

EQUIPMENT

- Black nigrosine stain
- Paint brushes
- Rags
- Rubber gloves
- French polish
- Lint-free cloth
- Nylon scourer
- Cork sanding block
- Soft brush
- Tack cloth
- Spray varnish (two cans were used on this little chest)

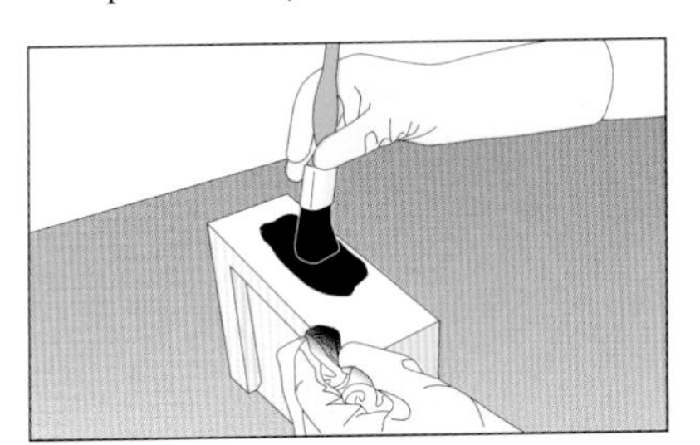

2 Apply black stain with a brush to a small area and immediately wipe off excess with a clean rag.

Applying oil finishes

Attractive timbers, such as the cedar used for the top and base of this little table, can be finished by rubbing in finishing oil. Traditionally linseed oil was used although a number of other oils are now available. Oil enhances the natural beauty of the timber and shows its grain, but it is not very resistant to stains and heat.

EQUIPMENT

- Abrasive paper: very fine grade
- Stain (optional)
- Rubber gloves (optional)
- Two paint brushes
- Clean cotton rags
- Finishing oil, such as linseed

METHOD

1 Prepare the item for finishing (see box on page 53), paying particular attention to achieving a fine, sanded finish (use very fine grade abrasive paper for the final sand). If you need to use a wood filler, make sure it matches the colour of the timber.

2 Stain the item or any parts of it that don't match. This is especially important when using an oil finish as variation in colour will be obvious. The leg and feet of this table were stained to match the cedar top and base. First, do a small test patch in an unobtrusive area (wear gloves if you like). Allow it to dry. If the result is satisfactory, brush stain over the whole area to be stained. If the stain drips or pools, wipe up the excess with a clean rag. Leave to dry.

3 Using a clean paint brush, apply oil to the whole item. As the timber soaks it up, apply more to any dry areas that appear. After about 30 minutes the oil should have penetrated well into the timber. This could take as little as 15 minutes on a

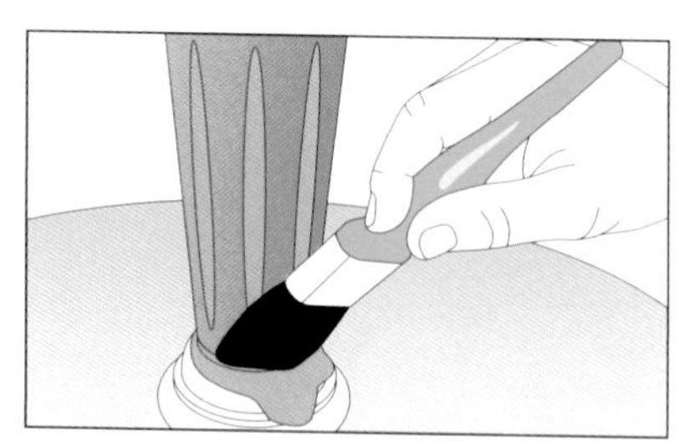

2 Stain any parts of the item that are made of different timbers so that the whole matches.

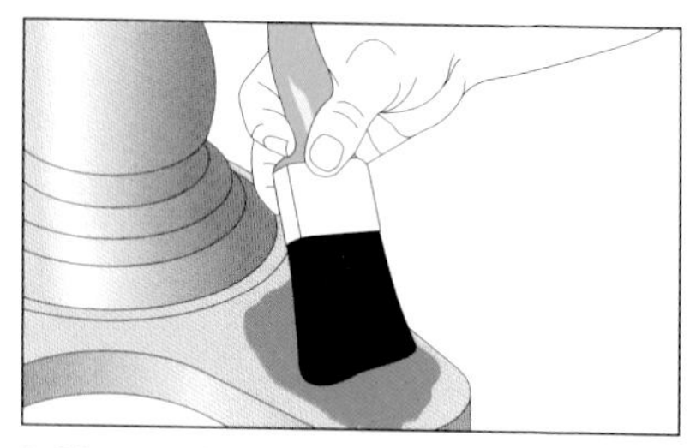

3 Use a clean paint brush to apply coats of oil over the whole item, applying more as it soaks in.

The leg and feet were stained to match the top and base of the table and the whole then treated with six coats of oil for a beautiful and easily-applied finish.

When stripped back, the top and base of this table were a beautiful cedar, while the leg and feet were turned from a paler timber.

hot day, or up to an hour in cooler weather. Before the surface becomes tacky, vigorously rub off any excess oil with a clean rag.

4 Repeat the oiling procedure a minimum of four times, for a protective finish, or up to six. The more coats applied, the richer the finish will be.

5 Over time, continue to rub in more oil, to maintain the appearance and to protect the surface.

CLEANING OILED FINISHES

Do not use furniture polish on furniture that has been given an oiled finish. To revitalise these pieces, rub wood oil sparingly into the surface, using a clean cloth and rubbing with the grain. To finish, buff over with a clean, soft cloth.

Stains and heat marks cannot be removed from furniture that has an oiled finish.

Tools for restoring furniture

Some of the most useful tools for restoring furniture are shown below. Build up your tool kit gradually—most of the tools can be purchased from your local hardware store.

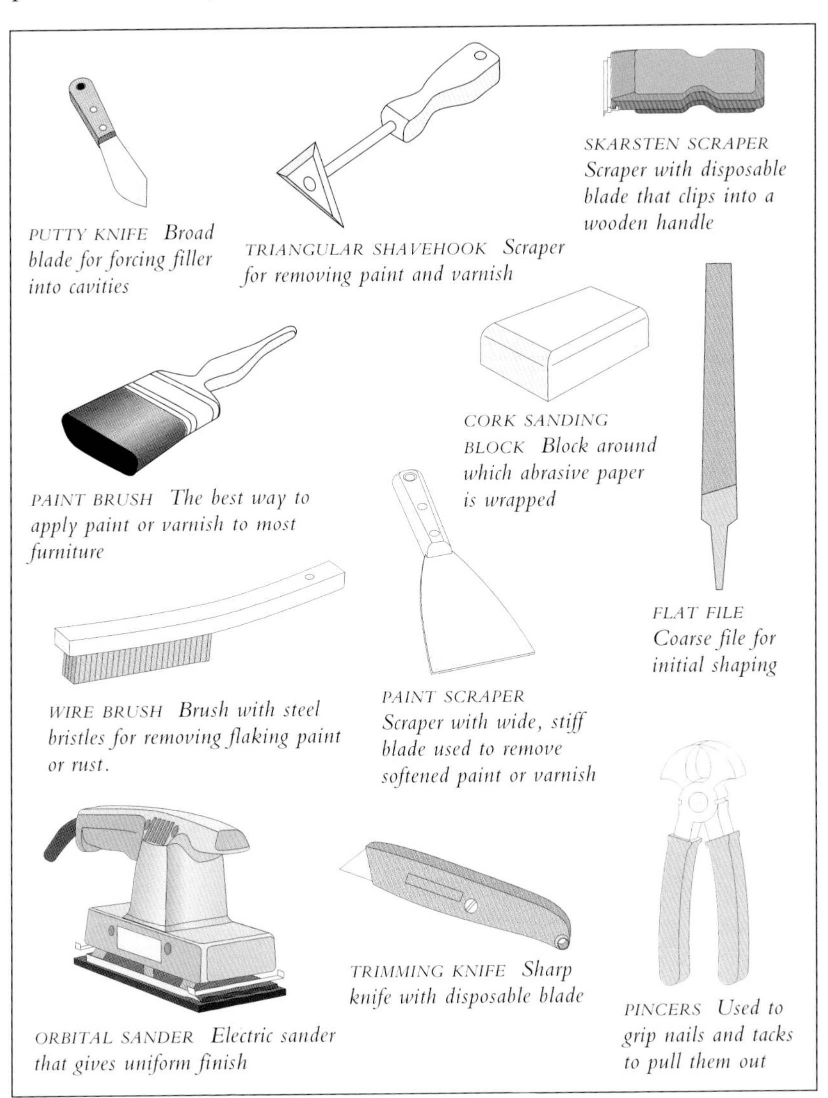

Index